The Solitary Voice of Dissent

Using Foucault and Giddens to Understand an Existential Moment

Martin Kay

VERNON PRESS

www.vernonpress.com

In the Americas:
Vernon Press
1000 N West Street,
Suite 1200, Wilmington,
Delaware 19801
United States

In the rest of the world
Vernon Press
C/Sancti Espiritu 17,
Malaga, 29006
Spain

Library of Congress Control Number: 2015948249

ISBN: 978-1-62273-091-9

Dedication

For my father
JOHN KAY, 1922-2014

Table of Contents

Preface

This book was written in the mid-west of Ireland and, initially, from a field of view that was limited to that general region. This is because my interest in solitary dissent started with my own experience, in 2014, of feeling an obligation over a period of time to reject the official account of a particular incident affecting part of the City of Limerick. Having recognised something distinguishable and worth exploring further, I then looked around me – and found a broadly similar sequence in the experiences of another who lived in Co Galway, just one hundred kilometres to the north.

Here, I need to say that I was always looking for written material describing a recent pattern of events and objection – in effect, a considered statement of evidence, something that could be repeatedly cross-examined in the same way that my own dissent had been declared and set down in print. This was, I felt, because people generally can be uncomfortable about engaging in oral interview and cross-questioning on deeply personal aspects of their lives and may introduce new barriers – whereas the voice in print, once impelled to speak out on the record, has no such inhibitions. The conclusions can then be made available to others, from evidence they can reliably interrogate in turn. It has to be asked, nevertheless, whether I was personally apprehensive, having already put myself out on a very public limb, about face-to-face encounters. Did I, for example, feel safer with investigation at arms' length? That is a valid thought to bear in mind because being a solitary dissenter is not comfortable. It is unsettling and a sense of fear in the background does not immediately die down. This may, in turn, induce artificialities to cover gaps in later reasoning. It follows that investigation at arms' length may work to advantage by tending to stabilise, by slowing the investigation down to a steady walking pace.

Before long, I began to recognise a common trait among solitary dissenters which did build my own confidence. They all appear to write as honestly as they can in order to defend their situation before as wide an audience as possible and to lighten the burden of their inevitable alienation from whatever context they can no longer support. Such candour is almost a self-preservation mechanism – to release the individual's accumulating upset by putting it firmly and respectably on the record and then attempting to move on.

This is very healthy and normal really, and probably consistent with the course of action any counsellor would advise the ill-at-ease to undertake. But what my case studies have revealed is also very accessible for being in this form and equally illuminating because it allows time for the reader to think and re-trace steps without losing any detail. It seems worth adding, too, that I was not attempting to deconstruct these written accounts but to get at the areas of concern or insecurity which caused them to be written. It was the separate approaches of Foucault and Giddens which ensured that my approach to those concerns was consistent.

Notwithstanding my attempt to remain rigorous and independent, however, I could not escape the fact that I was Case Study 1. There is, therefore, a methodological 'health warning' about my own account, which I comment further upon, and have attempted to contain, in Chapter 2.

My second Case Study, in Co Galway, was unknown to me personally although I was aware of his name and, from media reports, of a little about the difficulties he had been having. But whereas I was involved in community safety and council issues, he, being a priest, was involved in spiritual health and church issues. So, we were different types of people, which was a good thing, but essentially travelling parallel paths, which was even better. This priest was initially cautious but became supportive before moving on to more pressing issues in his fractured career. I have had no further contact with him.

In order to try and broaden further the basis for conclusions based upon these two, initial case studies, I began to widen the radius of research. I approached one ex-junior minister in Dublin who, by my estimation, had declared her solitary dissent from the actions of her departmental leader, a member of the Irish Cabinet. I was particularly keen to attract her interest in order to avoid accusations of gender bias. But I received no reply. To be fair to the lady in question who had lost her Party whip, she was occupied within her constituency with the imperative of retaining her seat as an Independent at the forthcoming general election.

Furthermore, I came to the conclusion that politicians were probably unreliable as raw material in an investigation such as mine: I sensed that there could often be an undisclosed agenda between the answers that might be given and the real reasons for declaring dissent. So, I deliberately avoided the class thereafter, persuading myself that lesser mortals, who lived their lives away from the public eye and had no need to 'gate-keep'[1], would be more candid and useful. I was not disappointed.

Very quickly, my search took me to London where I had been attracted by the plight of a senior journalist from a very well-known broadsheet. For a period, however, I could obtain no answer from him: I could neither find a point of contact or address, nor get a response from the staff of a magazine I knew he contributed to. Finding no other current candidates, I felt that the investigation had reached as far as it could. Suddenly, however, after some two months of silence, I received an encouraging email from my journalist, Case Study 3, by which time I had discovered, to my great delight, that he, too, had committed his dissent to paper and made it available to whomever wished to read further into a separation that had since become public knowledge. He was immediately supportive and remained so, although contact has lapsed.

The next difficulty was probing further into the consciousness than the written statement of dissent allowed. This is a limitation of my investigation which I have already flagged up: people are reluctant to engage in conversation about the deeply personal and have other distractions. Case Study 2, whose national profile was substantial, evidently had better things to do – and I was embarrassed about asking a man more questions about his early experience of a world he had ritually and professionally eschewed, than he had already chosen to answer. Case Study 3 had already gone as far as he needed to and, demonstrably, was difficult to contact. Furthermore, he evidently had a thriving social life (he captained an English cricket team which even played in Ireland) and his act of solitary dissent was, as far as I could tell, history to him and best consigned there. That left me, therefore, with my own personal baggage to sieve for other fine evidence – which actually served in the end to enrich the challenge of describing how to pin down the real reasons why a solitary voice has spoken out.

A fourth, stabilising 'leg' for my investigation did eventually arrive. I had been keen to take my search beyond Ireland and UK but could imag-

---

[1] Gate-keepers control access to benefits (information) they do not necessarily own, an exercise of power which has a value unfettered by production costs and can therefore be considerable (Corra and Willer, 2002).

ine excessive, perhaps insuperable, difficulties in identifying, accessing and then investigating the personal situations of personalities in the European continent or even further afield. The first difficulty would be identifying possible candidates, and the second struggling to get on to their individual agendas. In any event, my purpose had always been simply to say something meaningful about solitary dissent which could then start 'a wider conversation': I never meant to solve the problem completely for which I had quite inadequate resources.

Once again, however, there was a breakthrough. I was reviewing western understanding of the way in which hegemony works when I became aware of a contemporary of Gramsci called Ignazio Silone. I did not recognise the name at the time although I realise now that he was very well-known indeed in the years from World War I to II and beyond. His mission, it seemed, was to tell the free world that Italians were not instinctively fascist. The picture that began to emerge from reading about Silone was of a life of two halves, the first highly involved in politics and yet the second, if still involved, similarly characterised by dissent. Silone became the final 'fix' for me – a confirmation that my analysis of the ways in which Foucault and Giddens could help understand the reasons for solitary dissent had already been reproduced by another and put effectively to work.

As hinted earlier, it may be thought a further limitation of my investigation that all my case studies are male. I can think of female solitary dissenters (mostly dead) and comment briefly upon them in Chapter 2. I have actually known and worked extensively with one female solitary dissenter who took on the English criminal justice system in the 1990s but need, at this remove, to leave her in peace. I have no gender bias away from such courageous individuals.

I wish to thank Fr Tony Flannery and Mr Peter Oborne for their interest and for their willingness to be part of this study.

I need to thank my partner, Joan Collins, who endures my writing adventures and generally manages to work round them. And unusually, the clinical and support staff of Ennis General Hospital in Co Clare. They created considerable 'thinking' space for me, over three weeks in January 2016 as I recovered from illness. They tip-toed quietly around as work continued, keeping a protective eye on the corner of my room where I had set up my desk. In effect, they took ownership of the project, too. And their interest in me, in my health and in my work was greatly appreciated.

But I have to thank, mostly, the memory of my father, to whom this book is dedicated. He was a man of utter integrity in everything he did. He taught me his form of loyalty and, from an early stage, that we must defend the weakest wherever they are oppressed or downtrodden and whenever we find them. I don't think that he himself was ever found wanting although his patience might from time to time. I think it is something to do with the spirit of the age in which he grew up and lived his life – an age, incidentally, which overlapped with that of my Case Study 4. I do not think that we will see such people again.

M.K.

Chapter 1

Introduction

Despite the suspicion, if not disapproval, that it empirically attracts, "the singular importance of the principled dissenting voice" has captured the attention of at least the 2012-16 constitutional adviser to the Government of Ireland[2]. But the particular example she quotes lies within juridical history – and the solitary voice of the layman has had few such prominent champions since the days of Florence Nightingale (Palmer, 2001). Serious, contemporary comment on the north-west European experience of solitary dissent is rare. The internationally known and respected magazine, *Dissent*, now in its 61st year, has offered more a loosely defined 'strain of radicalism' for non-conforming ideas and for activists inclined to oppose, than a lens for examining this central yet neglected phenomenon. Indeed, it seems that the title of the magazine itself was something of an accident[3].

This short book sets out to fill this gap with detailed analysis of two recent examples in the Irish experience, of one more provided by a senior journalist in UK, and of one historical experience from the Italian political turmoil of the earlier 20th century. The endeavour is motivated by three principal factors and not merely by the desire to put the record straight.

First, there is the belief that management and administration, in our increasingly complex and inter-dependent world, might think it a sensible precaution to create some 'space' to fully concentrate on the solitary voice and not to set out instinctively to suppress it or side-line it. This belief grows into certainty as the book unfolds, not least because it can be argued from the evidence presented that there must inevitably be some sort of penalty when marginalising or otherwise moving against the inconvenience caused by the lone dissenter. He or she would not incur the stress

---

[2] *The Irish Times*, 24 June 2013 – interview with the Attorney General, Máire Whelan SC.

[3] Co-editor's newsletter, 'The political promise of little magazines', sent by email to subscribers, 1 December 2015.

and bother of dissenting if, from their specialist knowledge, they had not discovered that something was wrong – something which they thought serious enough to justify taking a stand. Lest there still be doubters, consider the dramatic, topical examples in Ireland of Garda 'whistle-blowing' and the 'Banking enquiry'[4].

Second, dissent being the exception, there is unlikely to be much detailed help for managers or administrators in how to set about evaluating the significance of the solitary voice. To be sure, complaints procedures may have been set up. But these, being the prescriptions of bureaucracy, may be more generally intended to smooth over the dissent, and to bring the solitary voice back into line while making suitably soothing, or perhaps even disapproving, noises. If bureaucracy cannot accomplish that, then the dissenter is transferred or 'let go'. The immediate problem may be solved but what about the underlying issue – and, of course, some further, eventual, adverse effect because the underlying issue has not been resolved?

It is not, however, an improved HR procedure or enhanced 'whistleblower's charter' that this book is offering but a way of understanding what may actually lie behind the situation that has suddenly blown up. It follows that the most efficacious remedy may not turn out to be dismissal: respect for the individual dissenting and careful thought about the implications of his or her dissent may prove a wiser, interim course of action.

And, third, it is a sad truth that the first of two great thinkers to give us the tools to enable this essential insight is himself too often side-stepped and the lessons of his work under-played. This is not because he is himself conspicuously a dissenter but because, for all his quirky Gallic appeal, he is too difficult to spend much time on. It seems too complicated knowing how to use what he has bequeathed.

Michel Foucault is notoriously challenging. It is hard work trying to get at what he is actually saying, especially as translations from the French may distort the underlying message. Consider, for example, the following,

---

[4] During the years 2011 to 2014, one retired and two still serving Irish policemen have separately spoken out about institutional malpractice and police dishonesty. In 2015, an unnamed civil servant provided an Oireachtas (parliamentary) select committee on Banking misdemeanours with evidence that they had been given incomplete information by the Banks themselves.

extraordinary and almost impenetrable sentence which is not, repeat *not*, characteristic of what you will be offered in this short book. The sentence, incidentally, is actually saying something intelligible, which will become progressively clearer through at least three of the case studies. But, oh dear, what an investment of effort and concentration it takes to be able to understand it:

> ... what I am attempting to bring to light is the epistemolog-
> ical field, the *episteme* in which knowledge, envisaged apart
> from all criteria having reference to its rational value or to its
> objective forms, grounds its positivity and thereby manifests
> a history which is not that of its growing perfection, but ra-
> ther that of its conditions of possibility; ...
> (Foucault, 2002: xxiii)

And that is the whole point. This book does not set out to make the reader reproduce such guff (however much it contains the essence of what Foucault is trying to tell us). Instead, it provides him or her with the best of Foucault, the parts they can use as thoughtful, observant executives or researchers, but stripped of his verbiage and opaque language. This is quite a helpful thing to do because Foucault is dead: no-one can go back and ask him to spell out more clearly something that is really not understood by lesser mortals.

The second great thinker, Anthony Giddens, is an English sociologist of huge reputation and, thankfully, still alive, accessible and intelligible. He is a British Life Peer whose writing has had a profound influence upon learning, society and politics across the world.

A connection between Giddens and Foucault is well-discussed (see, for example, Haugaard, 2016, and many more) – indeed, Giddens himself is thoroughly appreciative of Foucault's contribution to understanding administrative power and the centrality of the nation-state. But there are differences, too, for example in Foucault's treatment of agency (see, for example, Caldwell, 2007). This book does not try to knit a closer connection than others have agreed or to find divergence: instead, it shows how the separate theorising of these two great minds can be used alongside each other to unearth, to expose and to explain the solitary voice of dissent.

The approach resembles standing at a work bench on which a number of tools are laid out. There are two particularly well-worn tools suggesting frequency of use. One is labelled 'archaeology' (from Foucault) and the other 'structuration' (from Giddens). In the manner of the craftsperson, starting work with a block of raw material, the tools are liable to be changed as the properties of the raw material steadily emerge. If any pattern is apparent, it is that 'archaeology' tends to be picked up most during the early stages and returned to as the work progresses – and that 'structuration' becomes the preferred implement in the later stages of refinement. In other words, the tools do different things but, together, they achieve the required result. There are other tools too – for example, Foucault's 'power/knowledge' and Giddens's 'practical consciousness'.

Generally speaking, it is Giddens who calls out "Over here! Start digging here." Then Foucault does the heavy work of exploration and exposure. Next, Giddens takes over again, in order to explain what exactly has been found. To put it crudely, Giddens starts off like a water-diviner with a forked stick; then, Foucault offers a spade; and, finally, Giddens again eventually produces a fine sieve for the sediment that is exposed. However, the sequence is not rigid: like tools on the workbench, they can be used as the craftsperson's experience dictates. The craftsman's instinct may differ from that of the craftswoman but Foucault and Giddens will take them both to very similar fine detail leaving each sufficient scope for imagination and difference – to that essential, delightful, personal interpretation of what has caused the solitary voice to speak out.

Power itself will not make the solitary voice speak out. It is in response to the use of power that lies the impulse to dissent. And that requires further brief comment upon gender in order that it does not become a greater distraction than the scope for difference which I have identified above.

In the early stages of drafting this text, I noticed a quote in my partner's *Gloss* magazine from *The Irish Times* of 2 April 2015. The feminist activist, Gloria Steinem, is reported as saying: "We'll never solve the feminisation of power until we solve the masculinity of wealth." That suggests to me, whether her remark was historical or not, that Ms Steinem was distracted by the surface effects of power, by its outward face to the world. Foucault, in contrast, is concerned with what happens in *every* dimension of this universal phenomenon, wherever and however it occurs. I have yet to find many clues, moreover, that he was interested in, specifically, the gender of power. He himself would now be described as 'LGBT' and his thoughts, like his sexuality, appeared to have progressed far beyond the preoccupations and prejudices of that looming political distinction. He was certainly interested in the history of sexuality but that is not the same as gender. He saw in the history of sexuality the product of power relations, rather than innate differences between male and female stereotypes. Gender simply provided a context. He may have been looking in the same direction as Gloria Steinem, therefore, and at similar phenomena but I believe he saw gender as part of the discussion and not the cause itself.

The lack of treatment of 'gender', in general, and 'women', in particular, in Giddens's work has been noted (Clegg, 1997: 144). However, it is still possible to contrast him with Foucault and Steinem. Giddens's view of sexuality differed from Foucault's in that he was able to separate it from the purely disciplinary and to develop a nuanced explanation of intimacy in the relationship between a man and a woman. (Giddens should not be seen as resisting today's acceptance of homosexuality: he was talking, as was Steinem, about the male and female genders.) Sexuality was 'sequestered' within the privacy of family life as it developed and changed from the basic requirements for reproduction to far subtler relationships in modern domesticity and partnership. So, in contrast with Foucault, Giddens was not actually looking in the same direction as Gloria Steinem, however much their subject matter appeared to be the same.

This book has been written with two principal audiences in mind – the corporate professional (whom, for indexing purposes, I shall call 'management') and the researcher in social sciences (whom I shall similarly call 'academics'). I believe it will be helpful to each in different ways.

By putting Foucault and Giddens to work, management will be able to apply their explanations to any instance of dissent without having to declare it or even reveal it. That has to be a good thing: senior management would not wish to know that subordinates were being distracted by, or even wasting time on, sociological or structural complexities. Usefully, therefore, and with a little practice, Foucault's approach becomes a mental exercise that can be conducted like yoga, calmly and in a relaxed state of mind. Giddens's approach in contrast, is not so easily put to work but it is not impossibly difficult. It just requires a little more concentration. But when the situation under investigation has been digested and its intricacies understood as far as the team leader or manager needs to go, then he or she can make whatever decisions are appropriate to the wider situation, as he or she reads it. That, too, is important: Foucault and Giddens will not tell the team leader or manager what to say but he or she can be cer-

tain that, by using at least one of them, the situation will have been understood in most, if not all, of its necessary complexities. And if they really
needed to dig deeper than Foucault allows, then Giddens will provide
them with the tools. The relatively small investment of time and effort,
which this book invites its readers to make, in order to master the first of
these approaches, will therefore be very well worth it in the end. Becoming
proficient in the second will deliver greater rewards still.

For academics, the book achieves three aims. First, it opens a conversation on the phenomenon of solitary dissent. There does not seem to be
one at present. Second, it takes two aspects of Foucault's unique insight
into the use of power and demonstrates how effective the combination
can be when seeking to illuminate hidden nuances. And, third, it suggests
that Michel Foucault's 'archaeological' insight can be used as a natural
precursor to applying the theory of 'structuration' put forward by Anthony
Giddens. Both Giddens and Foucault are concerned with power but Giddens uses a subtler analysis to extend the investigation when Foucault's
'excavation' has done its work: Foucault shovels the unwanted stuff out of
the way while Giddens gets to grips with the exposed substratum. It needs
to be said, as well, that Giddens might not achieve the same results if Foucault had not completed the spade-work for him.

If I appear to allow more space to Foucault than to Giddens, it is because that is how the book has worked out. The greater part of the activity
has been Foucault's because that is where the empirical work took place.
Foucault has exposed what we needed to know about the solitary voice of
dissent – but it is Giddens who is capable of taking us further if we really
needed to dissect the individual consciousness acutely. Bringing Giddens
into this discussion at an apparently late stage is not a case of searching
for an 'exit strategy'. Giddens provides the essential explanation of ontological insecurity, which is where the motivation to dissent originates. It
follows that his place in the book is already secured because it is he who
directed Foucault at the outset to the best place to begin.

Clearly, not everyone needs to atomise their findings in the way that
Giddens ultimately enables but I do also suggest, for the researcher who
does, how such a task might be accomplished. Such ease of transfer (from
Foucault to Giddens) might also tend to make Foucault's approach a more
obvious addition in combinations of methods deployed in other research
projects. It should, furthermore, start a bell ringing in the sociological
memory. Did not Giddens once spend much intellectual effort in exploring the intensely private phenomenon of suicide? Could there be parallels

embedded in the literature of Foucault, who was also interested in suicide, and Giddens? And, if so, with what significance?

In Chapter 2, I review what is known about dissent in general and solitary dissent in particular. Group dissent has attracted prestigious interest – for example, from Hannah Arendt. But it is clear that no-one is particularly comfortable with the individual who speaks out and it will become apparent that few have cared to follow up 'group discomfort' at a solitary interruption by writing about it. It is in this Chapter, too, that I spotlight the striking relevance of Jean-Paul Sartre's existentialist thinking to dissent. Indeed, I draw further upon Sartre to explain how I have attempted to mitigate any distorting effect that my own involvement in interpreting my own evidence might have.

In Chapter 3, Foucault's approach is carefully explored using everyday language as far as possible. To be sure, his own, distinguishable terminology is preserved but this becomes progressively easier for the reader to understand and to use as the explanation continues. The discussion then moves on to Giddens and his approach to sieving the rough chunks that Foucault has unearthed. While Chapter 3 is methodologically slanted, it is also very much an explanation of the theorising of each.

In Chapter 4, the first example of solitary dissent is investigated. In Chapter 5, the second Case Study is examined; in Chapter 6, the third; and in Chapter 7 the fourth. Of the four case studies, Chapter 4 is the lengthiest one because it has the most material to work with. It becomes clear that Foucault's approach is particularly useful in Case Studies 1 to 3, with Giddens helping considerably in Case Study 1; and that the methods of Giddens and Foucault, together, are endorsed in Case Study 4 by two central personalities active in the tale. The first point is, as remarked in the Preface, that the implements provided by Foucault and Giddens are as interchangeable as different chisels when exploring and exposing the knots and whorls of a twisted piece of old wood. And the second is that some people have grasped the need for such implements and fashioned their own versions first.

In Chapter 8, the results are assessed and conclusions are drawn, and in Chapter 9 some ideas about the future tentatively expressed.

There are two rewards for reaching the end of this tale. First, the reader will understand the range and complexity of the issues that can prompt the solitary voice to speak out. And, second, he or she will suddenly discover a way of reliably exposing the local workings of power and understanding intimately why someone has chosen to object. One cannot dissent in a vacuum; one can only dissent from the use of power.

It is the message of this book that no-one can turn to Foucault without becoming sensitive to who holds power and why, irrespective of gender. All that will remain to be conceded is that Foucault is also telling us something about what they are doing with their power; and that Giddens can reveal the effect it is having upon people who stand in the way, and why. These two insights will make sense of the whole situation.

I wish to add, too, that reaching the end of this tale will help the reader decide whether solitary dissent is an issue academic enquiry should pursue further. And if the answer is 'yes', then one approach is elaborated here for those who take up that challenge and continue the conversation. I feel privileged to have taken the first faltering steps and offered some basic ideas.

Chapter 2

Exploring Dissent

Until it can be defined further, dissent means people standing up and saying "No!". The point about standing up is important. Those who continue in their seats and say "No." are generally declaring their rejection of whatever dissent has been raised. Their decision is final, there is no need for further discussion. The question of power, therefore, is central to any examination of dissent – and dissenters, whether group or individual, are all characterised by relative powerlessness.

Power is control: "the ability to constrain the choices of others, coercing them or securing their compliance, by impeding them from living as their own nature and judgement dictate" (Lukes, 2005: 85). In the next Chapter, we will see how Foucault takes this explanation much further – but, for the purposes of this Chapter, Lukes, who is an authoritative commentator, tells us all we need to know.

The next important point, after the distinction between standing up and staying seated, is the act of speaking out. Hannah Arendt explains how easy it is to disagree with what is being said or proposed – in other words, to feel like a dissenter – but actually to fail in the task:

> Dissent implies consent, and is the hallmark of free government; one who knows that he may dissent knows also that he somehow consents when he does not dissent.
> (Arendt, 1973a: 71)

So, let us now turn to those who look and sound like dissenters but may, for our purposes, be masquerading – either as radicals, reformers, resisters or simply dreamers.

Arendt shows us that dissent is not simply a 'couch exercise', a matter of preferring the liberal to the illiberal and doing nothing about it. But, equally, incomplete action, taken almost to the extreme of eventual radicalisation, leading possibly even to violence against the State (Cohen, 2005), is not dissent either: Cohen *nearly* became a revolutionary but didn't in the end. Nor is dissent the phenomenon of so-called 'dissidents' or non-conformist individuals prominent in their *milieu*. In 'underground movement' form, these were notably manifest, in the modern experience, in the sense that the Soviet invasions of Hungary in 1956 and Czechoslovakia in 1968 exposed (Lourie, 1974). In a similar way, in Irish memory, the activism and class struggle of James Connolly and the trades unionism of James Larkin in the early years of the 20th century might also have been characterised by observers of that period as 'revolutionary' and 'rebellious' or, in today's language, as 'radically reformist', but never as 'dissent'.

In more recent memory, however, there was the striking and moving example of Rosa Parks who, in 1955 in Alabama, refused to move to the back of a bus, where her coloured status required her to sit and where she was instructed to remove herself. But that was resistance not dissent: it was a deliberate, obstructive act against the laws of the State that, in turn, inspired a whole upheaval of a society: "I have a dream ..." as Dr Martin Luther King, who *was* a dissenter, would later put it.

Dissent is not simply academic disagreement – as, for example, in Mitchell Cohen's critique of Foucault's postmodern 'fumbling' of the reasons behind the collapse of the Peacock Throne (2002). It is not even celebrity *angst* – for example, the international campaigning of rock-stars or the cultural power of the famous and the glamorous (see, for example, Gitlin, 1998). But read on ...

At its very origin, dissent has to come from inside the individual and be of fundamental importance to his or her being or survival: declaring dissent must constitute a critical moment for the individual and be transformative. Jean-Paul Sartre was a relentless dissenter in the face of historical, social, political and economic constraints upon human freedom. He even dissented from the Nobel Prize that was offered him – and even from himself and his earlier thoughts, acts and writing. Notwithstanding this pattern of "inconsistencies and errors" (Aronson, 2013: xxii), Sartre, as an otherwise reliable champion of freedom, describes the 'certainty' of the moment of dissent as the individual's choice between a continuing void of oppression and, in the face of such peril, the personal triumph of being able still to reason out the word "No!" – and, significantly, *to commit to that declaration* (Sartre, 2007:36; Sartre, 2013a).

Perhaps certain rockstars do deserve to be excused their *angst* and readmitted as dissenters, then? The individual has to be impelled by something so antithetical to what he or she believes in or perpetuates in his or her way of life that the act of responding is as unavoidable as revulsion at the sudden discovery of the unspeakable affront in the first place. There must be plenty of local examples of this, serving also to emphasise that professional dissent is not the exclusive reserve of writers and philosophers. In *The Irish Times* of 2 January 2016, p.12, for example, there is a detailed obituary for one Paul O'Mahony "[an Irish] criminologist who argued for a humane justice system" and furthermore did something about it. The author of the obituary, citing a former colleague of O'Mahony, explains that "his work was academically rigorous but its core quality was always a seeking out of the truth, often the uncomfortable truth, and, most especially, *he spoke truth to power*" (*ibid.*, italics added). Another example, from my own experience, is Professor Bengt Flyvbjerg who spoke the truth about the urban planning culture in Aalborg, Denmark. Flyvbjerg (pronounced 'Flooberg') reappears in Chapter 8, below, as a point of reference.

The brilliant but tragic Rosa Luxemburg, who seemed to dissent from pretty much everything to both the right and even the left of working class struggle, spoke the truth like this:

> Freedom only for the supporters of the government, only for the members of a party – however numerous they may be – is no freedom at all. *Freedom is always … freedom for the one who thinks differently.*
> (Luxemburg, 1940, italics added)

Appropriately and helpfully, therefore, the Soviet writer, Andrei Amalrik, viewing that same hiatus in terms of 'freedom', suggested that the origin of this impulse lies between the individual and his or her conscience (Lourie, 1972). This book argues that Amalrik's explanation of such moments of isolated, individual, transformative judgement was accurate but can be further refined. Giddens, in particular, will approve for Amalrik's is completely consistent with his own explanations (see Chapter 3, below). The transformation is the conversion of growing inner anxiety into something liberating that can itself be expressed – a shift away from (concealed) ontological insecurity on to a platform that can and must be articulated.

"No. *No!*"

It is possible to identify several forms of authentic dissent. First, creative dissent.

The dissenting, questioning habit of the great American novelist, Norman Mailer, grew from early revolutionary socialism through non-conformism to constant critical rebellion. We might also include the young WH Auden, George Orwell and today's Ai Weiwei in this category, as examples of artistic brilliance challenging and confronting political indifference. In contrast, there is the witty, playful dissent of Voltaire who satirised the norms of 18th century Europe and its Establishment through the travels and adventures of Candide.

By way of extension, there is the professional dissent of later writers urged by Jean-Paul Sartre (2013b), who almost deserves a strapline to himself on the flyleaf of this book. *Detach yourselves from the accepted world of the bourgeoisie*, I can hear him insisting. *Live now, in the present, and make your impact upon the future you can change. If you fail in that, you will sink into the contemptible slough and mediocrity of contemplative relativism.*

Pablo Medina (2015), recalling the Cuban poets Padillo and Rivero, gives us many clues to the nature of dissent. Such solitary, creative dissenters as Padillo and Rivera were unlikely to have enjoyed, for example, the freedom, abundance and tolerance of life in New York that he, Medina, had enjoyed. Instead, what to write and what to think would have been prescribed. The individual's personal 'truth would have been suppressed by intolerance and the 'tyranny' of the 'truth' imposed by the system. Words would be the only weapons left in that clash with ideological intransigence and intellectual mediocrity and stagnation: "It is not that [Padillo and Rivero] sought out confrontation, but that confrontation was forced upon them. They wrote out of conviction that the individual right to say and write what one knows and believes is sacrosanct." Such themes have no ideological foundation but, citing a German poet, Novalis, Medina explains that they "arise instead out of [...a...] sober and spontaneous encounter with the world", an encounter which deeply disturbs some transcending passion and pure ideal. "It takes courage to speak the truth where truth is considered a threat."

So pure and simple dissent, we learn, is characterised by anxiety, transformation, truth, courage and freedom. That is an impressive crescendo and not something to be condemned out of hand.

Fatalistic dissent, being a somewhat subversive activity of certain people who labour, like the Cuban poets, under a disapproving regime, is closely linked to creative dissent but suggests that common sense and self-preservation may also moderate the ideal. Andrei Sinavsky (1984) describes fatalistic dissenters as "people who disagree with the system and have the courage to express themselves but often under a pseudonym. They do not consider themselves guilty of anything but recognise that the wage for their effort is imprisonment and that they will eventually be paid." Theirs is a low-level, partisan type of thing having "an heroic, romantic and moral aura" (*ibid.*: 155). A rather insipid form of dissent, you might think, when compared with the real thing.

To emphasise the difference, let us turn to principled dissent. Consider *A Man for All Seasons* and Sir Thomas More: he lost his head for his principles. And then there was Jean Jacques Rousseau and his *Social Contract*: his dissent underpinned the Enlightenment in France and continues to be relevant and respected (to a point) in social and political thought today. Rousseau's 'point', that man is born free but is everywhere in chains, needs brief elaboration from the perspective taken in this book. It was not a matter of being born free to squander man's heritage and potential, like Marcel Proust[5] whom Sartre dismisses (see, for example, 2007: 37 and 2013b: 137), but born free to engage and contest. *Take responsibility for those chains!* Sartre demands of us when we recognise our inclination to remain powerless. *Man will demonstrate that he is absolute* (as distinct from relative) "… because [he] will have fought passionately within [his] own era, because [he] will have loved it passionately and accepted that [he] would perish entirely along with it" (2013b: 134).

More recently, there are the examples from British political life: from the Democratic Left, the Labour leader, Michael Foot, and his contemporary Lord Longford, a passionate defender of liberty and those who had lost it. Both Foot and Longford were frequently dismissed in contemporary British thinking as 'no-hopers' (Foot for his ineffectual, political leadership and unimposing presence, and Longford for his support of the loathed 'Moors Murderer', Myra Hindley) but you could never doubt the strength and sincerity of their principles. In more recent years, the Irish socialist politician, Deputy Joe Higgins, has provided another example of strong principles and integrity transcending his elected position. There is also Roger Baldwin's example of lifelong opposition to tyranny, violence

---

[5] Marcel Proust was the, then, much fêted author of *A la Recherche du Temps Perdu*, which, if anyone who has tried to read its many pages will know, is trying in the extreme. I keep my 23 volumes, like literary bricks, to throw at those who think there is something more to them …

and militarism, and his championing of civil liberties (Haskell, 1982). 'Champion' is a good word: readers will be able to recall their own national examples.

Closely allied to 'champions' is political dissent – notably and already mentioned, Martin Luther King and Rosa Parks. Her early action was characterised more by resistance but she did subsequently pursue a life-long career characterised by loud, outspoken dissent. There is also the Indian example – particularly, Jayaprakash Narayan (or 'JP' as he was apparently known) who demonstrated the effectiveness and appeal of non-violent Gandhi-ism in the Indian sub-continent of the 1970s. JP was a veteran revolutionary socialist who confronted Mrs Indira Gandhi's ruling Congress Party and 'forced' the economic plight of millions on to the political agenda of the day (Judd, 1975).

The more one looks, the more examples can be found. Pierre Goldorf's experiences in Fidel Castro's prisons in the 1960s and 70s, having expressed (mildly and courteously) his disillusionment with the character of the emerging regime (Levi, 1978). Also Jean-Paul Alata's experiences in Guinean prisons at the same time (Faux, 1977). And, of course, the much reported and world-wide profile of the experiences, over 27 years in Robben Island prison, of Nelson Mandela.

From these might be distinguished 'Black Urban Dissent', as seen in the career of US Congresswoman Shirley Chisholm who served the American and Black communities of central Brooklyn in "a fiery yet *ultimately accommodationist*" way (in stark contrast to the methods of the two senators vying to replace her) (Sleeper, 1983, italics added). There may be parallels in today's ethnic recognition and human rights movements – dissent but mostly resigned acquiescence.

Clearly, political dissent has its limits and these may not be dictated by the colour of one's skin but by events and varying agenda. By way of a contrasting example, we might introduce here the phenomenon of radically chic dissent. Nicolaus Mills (1983) cites an earlier essay by Tom Wolfe describing a New York Park Avenue collection point in support of the Black Panther revolutionary movement.

And then there is civil disobedience, which seems closer to political dissent and more authentic for it. Civil disobedience entailed staying within the law, rather than breaking it in the sense that Rosa Parks demonstrated. One notable example of civil disobedience lies with Ignazio Silone, the founder of the Italian Communist Party who devoted himself to the struggle with Fascism and then, inevitably, Nazism. Silone is Case Study 4 in this book. Silone saw an immensely powerful tool in civil disobedience, if widely adopted. It was, above all, "a transformation of the spirit, a refusal to acquiesce to (*sic*) a regime that is contrary to reason and conscience" (2006). Silone was a self-proclaimed and demonstrable "partisan of democracy and liberty" (*ibid.*) and yet the basis of his teaching in Christian thought was deemed sufficiently dangerous and inimical by Moscow, to Stalinist plans for the spread of totalitarianism after World War II, to have Silone spectacularly betrayed and neutralised. More recently, there are the similar examples of Vaclav Havel, Gyorgy Konrad, Adam Michnik and others – political personalities at that point of clash and confrontation between freedom and oppression:

> ... in the conflict between totalitarian regimes and democracy you must not hesitate to declare which side you are on. Even if a dictatorship is not an ideal typical one, and even if the democratic countries are ruled by people whom you do not like.
> (Cushman citing Michnik, 2004).

From examples such as these, the themes of transformation, courage and freedom are reinforced – and something we can call for the moment 'conscience'[6], as the cause of anxiety and the impetus to dissent, introduced.

"No!"

In fact, one does not actually have to physically speak the word, as two striking examples of symbolic dissent make clear. First, there was the Tiananmen Square incident in Beijing where that courageous young man halted a column of tanks by force of his presence and personality. And a second, subtle but no less powerful example from China where dissenters reportedly place songbirds in cages (Siedelman, 1989). Symbolic dissent is not the exclusive preserve of the East: remember the empty pairs of shoes lined up around La Place de la République in Paris, after the November 2015 attacks by Islamic State and when *les citoyens* were forbidden to

---

[6] We shall see how Giddens takes the question of 'conscience' further in Chapter 4, in a discussion of 'practical consciousness'.

demonstrate by the state of emergency then in force. But for most purposes in the western experience, the solitary dissenter will actually say it.

There is an intellectual element to authentic dissent as we know it – a reasoning and inner debate based upon the ontological insecurity that is beginning to emerge. The Italian novelist, thinker and writer, Silone, Case Study 4, exposes this quality of intellectual dissent dramatically and movingly:

> It is terrible when God loses his patience and he cries out into the soul of someone; he begins to shout and command like a woman giving birth; it is something that cannot be recounted; it is something that must be experienced to understand what it means; to understand how, with that voice in one's soul, *one can forget even promises made to the police …*

We might read this in the following way[7] – that the inner turmoil can be such as to rupture ingrained civil obedience and the quality of being law-abiding (by way of explanation, Silone's status as a refugee in Switzerland forbade any political activity of the sort that Stalin manufactured against him). Silone continued by emphasising, for the purposes of his search for truth, how even-handed, honourable and fair his inner quest for truth became – almost as a deliberate, apologetic correction to this rupture:

> … In any case, I realize, in my high esteem for the authorities of this country, that in the painful struggle between the democratic police and democratic, political militants, the hardest role is not that of those who go to prison. *I am aware that to go to prison and suffer persecution for the sake of liberty is easier than to persecute and to imprison.*
> (2006)

---

[7] In fact, Chapter 7 will explain that Silone's words require a different interpretation, although the point about truth remains valid. The 'different interpretation' is a reflection of the life of two halves, referred to earlier.

This latter theme, of exposing for popular critique, the frailties, inconsistencies and difficulties of the status quo and reemphasising strongly the need to overturn entrenched practices, was echoed by Mitchell Cohen in his explanation of smart dissent (2014). Smart dissent "debunks but always seeks ways to make lives—or more generally, the framework of life—better". Cohen saw dissent as "a humanist venture and not a static one", an intrinsically left-wing activity championing the rights of suppressed liberty and equality. (In expanded form, humanist thinking emphasises the value and agency of human beings, individually and collectively: it prefers critical questioning to the unthinking acceptance of dogma and superstition. Self-evidently, humanism is close to Sartre's existentialism: he even delivered a world-renowned lecture in 1945 with both words in the title, which is included in the bibliography of this book.)

Cohen's reasoning, we are told, has been conditioned by the experience of Post-WW2 America – by McCarthyism, capitalism, the Police State, neo-conservatism and any other 'ism' that afflicted the vaguely socialist ideal. In similar vein, Herbert Marcuse, from the ex-Weimar Republic, the Frankfurt School and then America and the 1960s showed the left, in *One-Dimensional Man*, how any protest must commence with recognition of how impoverished and empty life had become under the notionally benign democracies of the West. Equally, the American writer and academic Michael Walzer understands dissent to rest upon debate and discussion, definition and defence (see for example, Walzer, 2013). For Walzer, it is an essentially group activity dependent always upon reasoned argument – which seems to reveal a passion for collective method rather than an individual reaction. We might term Marcuse's position pedagogic dissent and Walzer's procedural but they both still fall, it would seem, within the umbrella of intellectual.

It is worth noting that the procedural element in Walzer's position is strongly supported by Hannah Arendt. For Arendt, the crucial consideration lay in whether individuals could collectively make a transition from insecurity to dissent (1973b: 60) – a question of passion, courage, communication and 'in-betweenness'. (By 'in-betweenness', she meant speech, action and mutuality.) For Ó Broin and Kirby, the crucial consideration was a challenge for a vigorous, independent civil society (2009) – in other, similar words, people acting spontaneously together to articulate a freely agreed position.

In whatever way we choose to categorise it, this idea of procedure, progression, independence and collectivisation is still consistent with the dimensions of dissent that have already been identified above. But the solitary dissenter is, again self-evidently, driven by something distinctly more internal: he or she is condemned to a circular, silent debate until the moment arrives to speak out. Silone explained this movingly, above. Isaiah Berlin, in the 1950s, may have undergone a similar experience in his dissent from the decay of political theory but his situation did at least enable him to express his dismay publicly and at an earlier stage.

In a similar way to Berlin, Sheldon Wolin, a notable US, intellectual, political theorist, dissented from the treatment of political philosophy by mainstream political science. Writing in the 1960s, he surveyed politics' "tradition of discourse" which he considered that in Western hands had become anti-democratic and anti-political[8]. "Classical political philosophy and modern political economy emerged in moments of institutional crisis, when the reigning powers were becoming increasingly illegitimate and civil war was on the horizon. They sought, therefore, not to democratize politics but to close it off" (Marcus, 2015). For Wolin, therefore, dissent was public opinion borne of a sense of public safety, if not also public defiance – "the contestation, differences and disputes inherent in political life" (ibid.). This recalls the stance of Cicero in ancient Rome in, for example, his consular attack upon the dishonest subversive, Catiline. It is even closer to the words of Victor Hugo in 1870, when Prussian forces were advancing on Paris (Paris again!), recalled by Lara Marlowe in The Irish Times of 11 January 2016, page 1:

> To save Paris means more than saving France ... It means saving the world. Paris is the very centre of humanity. Paris is the sacred city. Who attacks Paris attacks the human race in its entirety ... I ask but one thing of you, unity! Through unity you will triumph!

The suppression of dissent was achieved through political organisation, in contrast with the encouragement of dissent through participation. So, pure dissent (that is, genuinely independent political thought and opinion) was denied a role in political life. Accordingly, Wolin devoted his life to academic research and supporting political activism by student

---

[8] Interestingly, it will be seen in Chapter 3 that 'discourse', by Foucault's explanation of discourse, could only become so.

interests: he was one of a number of democratic radicals "dispirited by the disappointments of the 1960s" (*ibid.*).

As we pursue inner turmoil and such disappointments leading to that moment of truth, we have discovered one or two key phrases and expressions. Transformational. Humanist. Championing. Defence. Liberty. Equality. Clearly, we are beginning to close in on a more sophisticated way of describing what is happening when the solitary voice speaks out. Husserl's phenomenology tells us that dissent cannot remain a hidden thing. Instead it must burst out: "All consciousness is consciousness of something" (Sartre, 2013a: 4; see also Flynn, 2006: 17) and an acknowledgement of Other. By his reasoning, it is a quality of 'intentionality' that must also be added to the mix – a consciousness of something in the world, as opposed to consciousness of nothing. A consciousness of nothing implies existence in a passive, vegetative state, whereas a consciousness of something implies engagement and the potential to contest. To put it another way, being conscious is a way of being in the world: being 'out of it' means … well, you take the point.

Jean-Paul Sartre found this quality of intentionality in existentialism, which sounds as if it has a left-bank (Paris again), rather dated flavour to it. To be sure, existentialism was associated with some leading philosophers of the earlier 20th century, a number of them French. But it has been argued that, despite being something of "a period-piece", it continues today as a respectable defence for the individual against the demands of mass communication and conformity (Flynn, 2006: 105). The idea will resurface buoyantly in the final pages of this book. Sartre explains that:

> … every object has an essence and an existence. An essence is an intelligible and unchanging unity of properties; and existence is a certain, actual presence in the world. …
> [In contrast with established thought,] existentialism … maintains that in man – *and in man alone* – existence precedes essence.
> (2013c: 88, italics added)

It follows that "man must create his own essence: … in throwing himself into the world, suffering there, struggling there, [he] gradually defines what this man *is* before he dies, or what mankind *is* before it [finally disappears]" (*ibid.*: 88, italics original). In other words, you stand up and say "No!" and define yourself for ever – or you stay seated, then slink away unheard of and of no particular consequence at all. Crucially, Sartre associates this existential moment with a pre-condition of "anguish"[9] and a "crushing responsibility" to do something about it: "existentialism is no mournful delectation but a humanist philosophy of action, effort, combat and solidarity" (*ibid.*: 91). And, as we are seeing from other examples, declaring dissent is, too.

We can see particularly how this happened in Sartre's own experience from Aronson's introduction to his selection of Sartre's essays and from his description of the moment in occupied Paris (it's that city again), when the tide turned finally against the Nazi occupation. After four years of silently saying "No", after four years of knowing that at some point or other each Frenchman and woman had at some point been in possession of information that could have condemned them to imprisonment, interrogation and worse, "after four years of repression and humiliation, Parisians [rose up] to demonstrate to themselves the power of their own freedom" (Aronson, 2013: xiii). In Sartre's own words:

> ... they wanted to affirm the sovereignty of the French people; and they understood that the only means they had of legitimizing the power of the people was to shed their own blood
> (*ibid.*: xiii, citing Sartre)

Truth, defining moments, transformation, life or death, freedom: "... they were doing what they had to do" (Sartre, 2013d: 116) in "...[an] explosion of freedom [... and ...] disruption of the established order" (*ibid.*: 118). Evidently, this business of dissent is a vital and empowering one but,

---

[9] It may be helpful to explain here that existential anguish is considered a technical term, meaning our "experience of the possible as the locus of freedom" (Flynn, 2006: 66). For Sartre, however, anguish is more red-blooded. It means "full and profound responsibility" to humanity to deliver Flynn's 'possibility' (2007: 25). Elsewhere he calls it "... anguish pure and simple, of the kind experienced by all who have borne responsibilities ..." (*ibid.*: 27). By way of amplification, Sartre offers the example of military leaders having to send people, inevitably, to their deaths.

for the solitary dissenter, life still can be tough and uncertain, and leave many questions to be answered.

So let us turn now to those questions in so far as they are dealt with in this book.

'Where did the following accounts of solitary dissent originate, and why?' is the principal question in this book. 'What combination of events and impulses caused the solitary voice to be raised?'

'Who is the author of that seminal moment?' is the next. 'And in the event that the author is not the person dissenting, can anything be said about the relationship between them?'

'Can any common factors between the following case studies and interviews be isolated and described?' will generate the conclusion. 'What can we learn from the evidence adduced and the methodology employed?'

If ever there was a case for using the 'first person singular' to explore such issues, then this is it. It is not comfortable, standing up when other witnesses retreat, because, in the context of this book, the person standing up has chosen to confront a greater power or organisation. As sociologists might say, only the 'I' can identify the start of that sequence and attempt to illuminate the inner consciousness that responded. Only the 'I' can ruminate this deeply in an effort to understand himself and his "point of anchorage" (Sartre, 2013e: 312-3, reflecting on Merleau-Ponty). And that is the technique I use in Chapter 4 to explicate the turmoil I experienced myself. There was no other alternative open to me. I could only speak *from* my inner turmoil and *to* my responsibility to confront its source – and you will have to take what I say with all the raw emotion it caused in me:

Since we are each of us ambiguous histories – good and bad fortune, reason and unreason – the origin of which never lies in knowing but in events, *it isn't even imaginable that we could express our lives … in terms of knowledge.*
(Sartre, 2013e, italics added)

The 'ground under the feet'[10] of the person now standing up is central, therefore, to understanding why some inner warning was ignored or over-ruled – and the ground under the feet has to be grasped in terms the sub-ject is comfortable about using, not language imposed by convention, discourse or other external authority. The more direct those 'terms', the better.

Even more interesting than the directness of the language used by the subject is the possibility that the potential for solitary dissent may be more widely dispersed. There may, just possibly, be a distinguishable trigger which can exceptionally override an individual's self-control and motor responses. Whatever this may be, it could lie latent within other people's inner consciousness, too, and might, without much warning, propel them into some other hostile spotlight's glare. That is an impulse which only the 'I' could attempt to put into words.

This investigation is post-modern in the sense that it shows how to de-construct both the silence that surrounds the impulse and the attendant crises and explanations. For Giddens, this was no more than a matter of modernity struggling with its unfinished task. But the text may be better understood, in view of the utility of Foucault's thinking to the questions set out above, as post-structuralist – a disruption of "the continuous chro-nology of reason" (Foucault, 2002: 9)[11].

Foucault's value lies in his relentless scrutiny of power, in his explana-tion of its further effects, and in his grasp of the significance of apparently random, raw events dispersed through time. To claim to be post-structuralist, however, might seem to be inconsistent with the central role announced for the 'I'. This is because Foucault sees such a personality as an historical construction (Bennet and Royle, 1999: 24), a creature of

---

[10] The phrase comes from Professor Bengt Flyvbjerg (1998: 222), in his exposition of the relevance of Michel Foucault's work to understanding local government planning practices, and is explored in Chapter 8 below.

[11] It needs to be said that Foucault himself would resist any label like 'post-structuralist'. For example, he lambasts certain French commentators for calling him 'structuralist' but is careful to avoid asserting, in the same sentence, that he is 'post-structuralist' (2002: xv). Foucault is, well, Foucault: he is simply his own obscure, difficult but brilliant self. (The commentators called him 'structuralist', incidentally, because he was concerned with the relationship or 'order' that might underpin outwardly unconnected events.)

structure and, therefore, laden with power-considerations. But it is the not-so-encumbered reader, still, who will have the last word once the actors in the following dramas have all had theirs.

It may be helpful to comment further in this section on 'structure'. In the sense used here, structure means something that is conceived, fashioned, developed, acquired and even learned – a 'rationality' that is created and reproduced in the way we lead our lives and in the choices we make. Such rationalities can be, for example, legal, economic, political or social (Gray, 1998: 17) and, being normative[12], will specify and, indeed, be structured themselves, by sanctions. Structures, therefore, whether they exist within the mind or within society or within a prescribed area for action, are the creations of power. The accompanying concept is 'agency' – the capacity of people and their potential for action in the spaces available to them. Dissent falls within the scope of agency, whereas the opposing power must lie within structure.

This is where Giddens comes in: Giddens is the master of structure and agency and his theory of structuration will emerge eventually as the complete answer to the problem.

To summarise the ground covered in this Chapter, we have seen that dissent is borne of powerlessness and yet also, if you do not declare your dissent, of the risk of continuing 'subjugation' (Foucault's word, as we will see in Chapter 3). It must follow, therefore, that even though your original powerlessness remains, the mere act of declaring your dissent is liberating in itself. In a moment of transformation, it brings freedom to the soul. And it is in the 'soul', or practical consciousness, that the anxiety began. That may be why some creative dissenters in particular have found it possible to continue incarcerated physically in prison having liberated their souls.

Freedom is more readily in sight for those who get together, articulate their concerns and reach a common standpoint. Indeed, that sense of doing something about whatever has led to their dissent is extremely em-

---

[12] This word 'normative' hovers above many of the ideas introduced in this chapter and needs to be grasped from the outset. 'Normative' means accepted and expected standards of behaviour within a given society. It follows that anyone who does not 'do it our way' immediately places himself or herself in a difficult position: anyone who dissents is going to find life 'interesting', as that old Chinese curse has it.

powering. A vibrant civil society is one way of describing their situation (provided that blossoming of the people's voice is uncontrolled, which is quite a separate debate), as they convert their inner anxieties into group strength and certainty. But freedom is a vastly more elusive thing for those who remain standing on their feet, the sole objectors to whatever has been decreed or imposed by those with greater power. Their anguish is condemned to twist and burn for longer still – and yet, we learn from very prestigious comment, something approaching liberation can still be found in that moment of certainty, courage and speaking out, whatever the consequences. For the solitary dissenter, it is a question of being true to yourself and to everything you stand for. Those who turn away without raising their voice are even going so far as to deny their very existence.

The Chapter was able to isolate a number of forms of authentic dissent – for example, creative, professional, fatalistic, principled, championing, political, the radically chic, the radically black, the radically smart, civil disobedience and even silent, symbolic dissent which we cannot deny can rise in beauty above the tragedy of it all. We shall note, in Chapter 4, that it is also possible to imagine environmental dissent. And, in addition to my environmental dissenter, Rachel Carson, I can certainly think of some other courageous women who have dissented in their various different fields – for example, the (then) Constance Gore-Booth, Martha Gelhorn, the (then) Mother Teresa, Mary Robinson and so on. And simply to be provocative, I personally do not think that Simone Weil, Simone de Beauvoir, Erica Jong or Germaine Greer did.

There will be more categories of dissent and much debate about them but however more and however much does not really matter. It is the integrity of the process leading to dissent that is important, a process which can be so overwhelming that it changes ingrained practice and habits. It will lead the individual through inner turmoil, to a progressively clearer consciousness that something must be confronted, to a moment of existential significance. In the words of the great existentialist, Jean-Paul Sartre, you start with 'anguish' and end up with a 'crushing responsibility' to do something about it.

The next Chapter will show us how to discover more about that anguish and how to pin it down for analysis. The Chapter turns, first, to Foucault and, second, to Giddens. As already hinted, it also signals and justifies a greater degree of intimacy in Case Study 1, through use of the first person singular, than we might normally expect. Given Sartre's crackling endorsement of the path the solitary dissenter is bound to tread, it could be no other way.

Chapter 3

Foucault and Giddens

The names of the dissenting actors in the case studies in this book could not have been as widely known as those of the powerful agencies ranged against them. Foucault explains this imbalance by contrasting continuity with discontinuity. The powerful agencies represent continuity, the dissenting actors discontinuity. The interruptions of discontinuity have since been lost from sight because they did not fit in with the expected view. He calls the approach needed to subsequently uncover them 'archaeological'. This general idea of sifting down through the sediment of history is a recurring and ultimately helpful metaphor in understanding Foucault's work. It is worth keeping it in mind as the following pages take us round and round, in Foucault's own habitual style, the central problem of power. In effect, we are excavating a hole and exposing more of the underlying conundrum as we do so.

We are accustomed to thinking about the past from this same historical perspective but we tend to think 'along history' or 'across it', rather than 'down through it' in Foucault's archaeological sense. This is because, so Foucault tells us, an historical reconstitution of events in the past prefers continuity, which it finds easier to deal with, to discontinuity. Those making the reconstitution incline to the narrative of powerful agencies, treating the people who stand up and say: "No!" as unhelpful, forgettable anomalies (Foucault, 2002:9). It is possible to bury the anomalous as time passes, just to get it out of the way (which is why you may have to dig down for it later). It follows that a general history emerges from historical reconstitutions which privileges the continuous. This general history provides a 'bloc' representation of coherent events and surface effects, 'slabs' of continuity which have been purged completely of local 'erudition'.

By 'erudition', Foucault is referring to the situation of these same people who stand up and say "No!" He is telling us that they know something, that theirs is not a frivolous interruption to be hidden out of sight, but something thoughtful and reasoned out, something erudite and deserving attention. But he also understands a lower-ranking knowledge still – a mix of local prejudices and experiences, incapable of unanimity (and condemned, therefore, to permanent powerlessness). This lower-ranking, essentially local opinion is immediately ruled out of any relevance to his-tory and its reconstitution (*ibid.*: 82) because of its untidiness and possible incoherence. But Foucault's point is that this lower-ranking knowledge still retains the potential to be relevant.

Foucault calls both the erudite and the lower-ranking versions 'knowl-edges' in the plural, in contrast with our habitual reference to 'knowledge' in the singular. He treats them as discrete phenomena whereas our use of 'knowledge' in the singular implies something that is homogeneous, smoothed-over and society-wide. Foucault's point is that authentic knowledge is particular, popular and locally relevant rather than general and serving to sweep aside everything else. It follows that to ignore all but the central, official, historically reconstituted knowledge is to suppress the others. By extension, therefore, to talk 'knowledge' rather than 'knowl-edges' is to acquiesce in the power of continuity. Foucault, in contrast, concentrates on these local knowledges which he says are "subjugated" (Gordon, 1980: 81, translating Foucault's words): the interests of the con-tinuous have "disqualified [them] from the hierarchy of knowledges and sciences" (*ibid.*: 82). And that hierarchy he identifies with the structures and disciplines that come from established power.

Necessarily, the habit of structuring history allows its twists and turns, its development through agency, popular knowledge and the interrup-tions of people who say "No!" to slip through our fingers and stay general-ly unnoticed. It becomes too difficult, or even too inconvenient, to articu-late a theory of discontinuities, because historical analysis prefers the dis-course of the continuous (Foucault, 2002: 14). It follows that an approved point of view, a particular historical perspective, becomes distinctly, if not also formally, privileged. And that point of view is firmly identified with the normative conventions associated with established power, not with annoying interjections from little people who say: "Stop!"

Remember how we were told in Chapter 1 that power is control: "the ability to constrain the choices of others, coercing them or securing their compliance, by impeding them from living as their own nature and judgement dictate" (Lukes, 2005: 85). Well, the 'normative conventions' referred to in the paragraph above can be described in one word – 'dis-course'. Discourse is "a local social order which allows one to say certain things but prevents others from being said" (Haugaard, 2000: 36). Clearly power and discourse go hand in hand.

It is possible to explore discourse, as rationality and meaning, from dif-ferent perspectives – for example, through structures, systems and symbols.   But when examining the way in which meaning is constructed and reproduced by actors engaged in social practices, it is inescapable that the power to generate meaning is "embedded in and effectuated through a crucial combination of knowledge and language" (Goverde *et al.*, 2000: 14).   Viewed as knowledge and language in combination, power can only facilitate what is said and offer no guarantee as to the validity of what the ensuing discourse allows (Fox, 1998: 416).   This is why some people can sometimes feel impelled to say: "No! I cannot agree! I must dissociate and distance myself from what you are telling me to believe."[13]

This interpretation was famously articulated by Foucault for whom discourse is a normalising process – "the ordered set of discursive practices" associated with a particular process or institution (Fairclough, 1995: 12).   In this context and as argued above, Foucault was exposing the structuralist preference for privileging continuity over that which might suddenly disrupt it (2002: 27).

Power operates externally upon discourse – through structures of prohibition, of division and of truth.   It operates internally – through hidden meanings, through author associations and through understandings of what may or may not be said.   Power also operates upon the speaking subjects themselves – through ritual, doctrinal and social practices (Sheridan, 1980: 121).

By Foucault's reasoning, it follows that the power which sustains discourse can be distinguished from the power which maintains the space for discourse to operate. (This may seem a strange distinction to make but its importance will become clear.) The former is styled 'discursive practices', the latter 'discursive relations' (Foucault, 1972: 45; and O'Farrell, 2005: 80 and 84, quoting Foucault). Discursive relations *delimit* discourse in the sense that they express its interface or relativity with neighbouring processes. Discursive practices are *limited by* discourse in the sense that their

---

[13] This whole paragraph is quite important. The reader might care to reflect for a moment on the experience of 'the troubles' in Northern Ireland and on the opposing perspectives of the Republican and the Loyalist points of view. Think about the totality of it all, from nationalist communities, to barricades, to gable-end art, to burning tyres, to guns, to Lambeg drums, to parades, sashes and so on. (If the reader wants an example outside Ireland, think of Hitler's Germany and the symbols and posturing of National Socialism.) And then, whichever example is preferred, read the paragraph above once again giving it careful attention.

meaning is generated by the power within. Examples of each are given in the following pages, although those who recall the corporatist sharing of power that underpinned the years of Ireland's National Development Plan 2000-6 may be able to identify their own[14].

The distinction between discursive practices and discursive relations also enables Foucault to compare *discourse*, as both the beginning and the end of power, with *domain*[15]. Domain is what is liberated when discursive practices are shattered and stripped of their trajectory (1998: 307). This chapter argues by extension that domain – "the *pure* description of the facts of discourse" (*ibid.*: 306, emphasis added) – is at the core of solitary dissent, and discursive relations may well form part of it. In contrast, discourse, where pure description is masked by the further effects and practices of the power within, is a condition that the majority of participants, once interrupted by the solitary voice of dissent, then consolidate and

---

[14] The years of NDP 2000-6 were characterised by an arrangement of dominating interests called 'Social Partnership'. This was a form of negotiated governance producing a sequence of national agreements (Adshead, 2006). For the purpose of demonstrating Foucault's definition: the *discourse* was economic recovery; the *power within* came from the government (specifically from the Department of An Taoiseach); and the central *discursive practice* was Social Partnership. But then consider the various 'pillars' of Social Partnership – the employers and business, the trades unions, the farmers, and the voluntary and community sector (or social pillar). Notwithstanding the assumption of parity between all pillars, the social pillar experienced exclusion from the policy community of Social Partnership, while the other three began steadily to grow their own power in the way that *discursive relations* are understood. Even the highly respected Combat Poverty Agency fell victim to this process.

[15] 'Domain' was something of an obsession for Foucault. In his hugely popular book *The Order of Things* (well, the book was popular in France), he calls it a 'middle region', something that lies between science and culture, between the ordering of codes and reflections upon order itself: "the most fundamental of all … the pure experience of order and of its modes of being" (2002: xxiii). He has a point: somewhere in the middle between power-interests and power-effects will lie a lacuna, a gap, an opening, a break in continuity, a rupture of everything they've been saying, and a glimpse of the real hiatus underneath.

perpetuate after discursively sharing their consciousness, their disapproval and their annoyance[16].

Foucault goes further – and we need him to go further if the nature of one very powerful discursive relation, identified in the example of Case Study 2, is to be fully understood.

If the external 'surfaces' of discourse expose and facilitate the practices within, then discursive practices and discursive relations are intrinsically different. The ordering of objects within discourse (discursive practices) is a dynamic and self-sustaining process (Foucault, 1972: 44). Once initiated, it goes on until the power dies or something shatters whatever the discourse has become at that point in time. If the power within is extinguished, then discursive practices must cease, too (see footnote 18 below for an example). But discursive relations can have further meaning: if they have accreted in the meantime sufficient power to sustain themselves, they will continue in their own right. Foucault sometimes called discursive relations 'externalities'. The phrase does not derive from any French usage beyond Foucault himself but, through its resemblance to the French word *externe*, meaning external or exterior[17], usefully conveys a sense of peripheral agency, something which comes from outside but feeds and grows off the power within.

Fox sounds a note of caution about accepting Foucault's explanations unthinkingly (1998: 417) but does concede that, by Foucault's reasoning, discursive practices run more deeply than the surface meanings of a particular domain. In this way, Foucault's 'archaeology' of knowledge becomes a truly compelling metaphor (Gordon, 1980: 85) and not just his

---

[16] I have direct experience of this phenomenon – at a conference on public private partnership procurement in Dublin in 2001. With the benefit of 8 years' experience of the PPP method and of the British Private Finance Initiative on which it was based (probably more than anyone else there), I asked where and how the discourse of economic and social infrastructure renewal had sought the involvement of the people who were meant to benefit. The reaction to this question, which I asked of several contributors, was unpleasantly disproportionate, the dislike palpable. The reason was that none wanted to know about small people who stood in the way: this was a high-earning, power-game and they only wanted a slice of the action.

[17] Larousse explains *externe* as "*qui vient du dehors ou qui est au-dehors*" (something which comes from outside or is outside).

personal fancy: Foucault seeks to expose "the seams in the rock" on which the actors stand, rather than the processes by which those seams got there (1972: 138). Archaeology is concerned with whatever the seam comprises – with whatever discourse consists of at that point in time but without its discursive trail which is inevitably dominated by power (1998: 306). What Foucault calls 'power/knowledge', which is *not* necessarily a negative connection, is actually the link between that which is discursive and that which is not – the means of excavating the solid ground beneath a given actor's feet and making available, 'genealogically', the resources found there.

Genealogy means the common memory, between erudite knowledge and lower-ranking popular knowledge, of their shared "historical knowledge" of struggle (Gordon, 1980: 83, directly translating Foucault's words). In everyday language, this might mean: "What we did and what we learned when we tried to fight it out all those years ago" – which is something that the structural approach to history will have long since buried out of sight. Foucault says that genealogy can be used today as "[an] *insurrection* of knowledges … against the effects of the power of a discourse that is considered to be scientific" (*ibid.*: 84, italics added). By "scientific", Foucault is referring to power that has been privileged – to strata of institutionalised, specialist power or slabs of continuity.

A useful example lies in his well-known examination of the power and establishment, over recent centuries, of the medical profession in its treatment of mental illness (Foucault, 1965; see also Gutting, 2001, and O'Farrell, 2005). Within those coherent slabs of respectable, continuous thought, of scholarship, medical and clinical practice, the embedded disciplinary mechanisms actually invaded the rules and expectations of individual social and legal rights and of 'sovereignty' (Gordon, 1980: 107). And by that, Foucault means that what the doctors and their clinicians decided to do has, with time and entrenchment, *lawfully* overridden the independence, reasonable expectations, self-respect and sociability of the individual. The individual can no longer say "No, I will not allow you to invade my privacy in that way", without incriminating themselves. Acts of assault and even battery become privileged and lawful by virtue of the perpetrator's position and authority and, crucially, by virtue of his superior, scientific knowledge.

How this actually happened can be seen in the following summary of Foucault's important research. Note how the condition of mental illness is initially located within society as an essentially human condition; then it moves out beyond society and away from humanity; and, finally, is assimilated once more within the human condition by more modern understanding and concern. The point is, however, that medical power and clinical perspectives change their intrinsic nature as that 'return journey' unfolds.

Until the mid-seventeenth century, mental illness was seen as an *essentially human condition*. It was opposed to reason. It existed as an alternative condition. But however uncomfortable, it could still be engaged with. From then until the end of the eighteenth century, however, mental illness was treated as a phenomenon *beyond human existence*, "a plunge into animality that had no human significance". This shift in perspective attracted moral condemnation of those afflicted – a stigma which persisted from the nineteenth century onwards. "[...*Once more...] within the human community*, they are [nevertheless still] seen as moral offenders, violators of specific social norms, who should feel guilt at their condition and who need reform of their attitudes and behaviour" (Gutting, 2001: 266, emphasis added). Reform is achieved through isolation and control which, crucially, is exercised on society's behalf by doctors. It is normal that doctors should manage the situation of the sick but, however much their 'care' may be camouflaged clinically, they have now come to do so from a position of moral authority not medical succour.

It follows that the meaning of normalisation can be developed. Power may characterise discursive practices but it accretes to discursive relations. It grows outwards from discourse and impacts upon the externalities, while strengthening inwardly and normalising whatever the discourse is saying. In this way, those pre-eminent in the discourse – in effect, those who do its work rather than those who preside over it – begin to exercise a moral domination over those expressing their ontological insecurity. Those whose function is technical and are not accountable for the power at the centre of the discourse, begin to '*ab*normalise' and even stigmatise those who normatively [express their dissent] (McNay, 1994; Sheridan, 1980).

This abnormalisation and stigmatisation, which together constituted an invasion of the sovereignty of the individual, brought about the circumstances for a hierarchy of power. Genealogy implies, therefore, the reactivation of local knowledge and of that which was discontinuous – the "tactics" whereby subjugated knowledges can be brought back into play *despite* that hierarchy (*ibid.*: 85).

There is only one central idea in Foucault's genealogy, claims the authoritative Lukes who is utterly weary of going round and round in circles like this: "...if power is to be effective, those subject to it must be rendered susceptible to its effects" (2005: 90). But if ever a statement could be guaranteed to provoke a sudden break in the flow and logic, it is this neat, academic axiom which seems disruptively dismissive and wide of the mark.

Lukes misses at least one point which, for the purposes of this book, lies in the reactions of witnesses to the way that power works. And here, Foucault, however convoluted and opaque his explanations may seem, is saying much more than Lukes allows. We should persevere, therefore, with Foucault's constant manipulation, testing and peeling away of this phenomenon (power) which seemed always to absorb him[18]. Persevering will demonstrate that 'genealogy' and 'discourse' are at least on a par with 'subject susceptibility' and are valid tools for understanding the motivation of individuals who disrupt – individuals who give voice to their powerlessness by expressing their dissent.

In sum, genealogy and discourse entail grasping the precise meaning, connections and exclusions leading to those solitary acts of disruption to continuity – the *specific* context in which each disruption occurred (Fox, 1998: 30). Only power/knowledge can satisfactorily illuminate that domain, that pure description of the facts of discourse once the discursive practices generated by the power within that discourse have been shattered and stripped away. Something in that domain gives rise to the actor's dissent. It remains to be seen whether that 'something' can actually be exposed and described – but at least we now know where and how to set about finding the answer.

---

[18] This cannot have been solely a mature obsession which Foucault grew into. A central recollection of Foucault's teenage years was watching German troops marching past the gate of his French home. His family was critical of Vichy France and he cannot have been insensitive to the way that power accreted to, and was exploited under, the Pétainiste *régime* that lasted until 1944. Following the Allied Invasion, Vichy France immediately fell. And with that extinction of 'the power within', the discursive practices of the Pétainiste *régime* fell, too. The *régime*'s discursive relations appeared not to last long either although, by Foucault's teaching, they could have done if they had acquired sufficient power to survive the wrath of the Free French people. Perhaps some did ... (On the latter point, see Lara Marlowe's article in *The Irish Times*, 9 April 2015, entitled 'Le Pens at war as daughter openly opposes father', page 11).

Let us turn now to dissent which, by comparison, is simpler to deal with.

Dissent is an early outward expression of non-acceptance. Its origin lies in ontological insecurity, which is both a crisis of self-identity and a failure in the constancy of the individual's social and material environment for action (Giddens, 1990: 92). Ontological insecurity is triggered when external power cuts across some "ultimate value or life meaning" (Löwith, 1993: 66) still preserved within the 'iron cage' of existence (Weber, 1930: 181).   Dissent is not coterminous with ontological insecurity because individual fear leading to discursive consciousness is, in the absence of dissent, initially marked by consent, as Hannah Arendt reminds us once again. At some point, however, the advance of ontological insecurity may incline those experiencing it to articulate their change of mind: if you are not actually dissenting then you are consenting (Arendt, 1973: 71).

Dissent can be traced to practical consciousness, which Giddens calls *tacit*, or personal, knowledge[19] about social life, as distinct from discursive[20] consciousness (1984) – and also to individual knowledge (Clegg, 2000: 82; Penttinen, 2000: 206). But it develops as the conversion of unsatisfied concerns into a preparedness to confront the power which caused the ontological insecurity in the first place.

Dissent, then, follows consciousness of the domain – that is, "the pure description of the facts of discourse" (Foucault, 1998: 306) which lies at the core of the ontological insecurity. If the actor only confirms his or her ontological insecurity, he or she continues to consent. We find ourselves, therefore, at a fork in the road but with the option, still, to turn back: behind us lies acquiescence and submission; to the front and on one hand, we have the 'in-betweenness' of a vibrant civil society and, on the other, the anguish of the solitary individual.

---

[19] Another way of describing tacit or personal knowledge could be 'unspoken': we know something instinctively but we don't need to talk about it because we already understand it; if we did need to talk about it, it would become discursive in the sense of footnote 20 below. But then it wouldn't be our own, personal knowledge anymore – it would be shared and the particular subtleties of personal knowledge would no longer be exclusive to its owner.

[20] Here, Giddens is using 'discursive' in the conventional, non-Foucauldian sense – the way we usually find it used.

The dual premise of this book is that solitary dissent is as authentic as collective dissent and, therefore, that authentic dissent can exist separately from civil society: it does not need to rely upon the support of anyone else for validity. Only the 'I' can explain what motivated what Sartre called 'man's absolutism' – and, at this point, we turn to Giddens to understand how.

For me, Giddens is something of a novelist, while Foucault is an intellectual flamboyant. Giddens is an acute observer of people and society. His understanding and his field of vision are quite different from Foucault's. Consider, for example, Giddens's very interesting, informative and accessible comments upon 'structure'.

He explains (Giddens and Pierson, 1998) that the structural properties of society impact upon the way that people act, feel and think. However, these same structural properties are not physically composed in the way that we understand the fabricated world around us. Instead "they depend upon regularities of social reproduction" (*ibid.*: 77). But even the reproduction of language is fixed, too. It is not possible break the tiniest convention of the English language without provoking a strong reaction from those who feel they have a greater understanding. And yet these same understandings only have form in the way that they are repeated in writing or speaking. That applies in social life, too: "… society only has form and that form only has effects on people in so far as structure is produced and reproduced in what people do" (*ibid.*). For Giddens, this model applies across society from the smallest level to the greatest.

Foucault could never have produced an explanation like that – he would have lost us before we reached the principal point which is that, however absolute, the 'I' never really stands alone but is still part of a social context which participants revalidate and reproduce as part of their daily lives. Clearly, the act of revalidation is both individual and collective, whereas reproduction is collective – a 'stew' of erudite and lower-ranking knowledges, as Foucault might have put it. But no-one can make a stew without having something to put it in – and that is where structure comes in.

Giddens's re-thinking of structure found expression in his theory of structuration. Its key lies in 'recursive implication' – or what people produce and keep reproducing in their daily lives. Structuration means the normative power of practical consciousness, grounded in the *duality* of structure and human agency and recursively implicated in the reflexive monitoring of interaction (Giddens, 1984). Note duality, not dualism.

We mentioned practical consciousness in Chapter 2 and identified it as the source of ontological insecurity: it is that part of the individual's consciousness not immediately accessible to discourse (Giddens, 1987: 63). In other words, you can't close it off, you can't escape it, its voice is always there in the background disturbing your sleep – and no-one else can get at it either. You can only attempt to suppress the gnawing anxiety it induces, with eventual consequences for your health and well-being, or else you can allow it to come out.

"No!"

By structure, Giddens understands rules and resources, or sets of 'transformative' relations, reorganised as properties of social systems. Systems themselves are reproduced relations, organised as regular social practices. Thus, structure is recursively implicated in social systems comprising the situated activities of human agents across time and space. This means that, normatively, the "structured properties of social systems can be stretched away in time and space beyond the control of any individual actors" (1984: 25). In this way, structuration describes the conditions governing the continuity and evolution of structures and also, therefore, the reproduction of social systems themselves.

The attraction of structuration theory lies in its consequent propositions. If the most important features of structure are rules and resources, then structural practice expresses *both* domination by rules *and* power from resources. But rather than view these as a dualism, Giddens insists upon their duality, in that rules and resources drawn upon in the production and reproduction of social action are *at the same time* the means of system reproduction (1984: 18). Moreover, the structural properties of social systems are *both* the medium *and* the outcome of the practices they recursively organise. Therefore, structure is not to be equated solely with constraint but is *always both constraining and enabling.*

Giddens's careful re-statement of structure and agency is that same arrangement which lies within the individual consciousness that Foucault helped us expose. But Foucault thought more in terms of power relations or constraint and therefore limited his prescriptions to unspecific 'insurrection' – which seems to me quite different from the 'enablement' of Giddens. It needed a painstaking novelist to explore and articulate such a finely balanced platform for greater possibilities in social life. In the meantime, Foucault, who left us with pages and pages of the ramifications of *episteme,* has long since moved on to extend our thinking in other grand ways and to pull down more of man's self-imposed boundaries. To me,

Foucault seems more like a visionary architect – a Frank Gehry[21] to Giddens's Anthony Trollope[22]. To put it another way, Foucault can unearth the way to *The Small House at Allington*[23] but only Giddens can show us how to get inside and how to make sense of the situation found there.

It is my conclusion, after a decade of thinking about Foucault on one side of me and Giddens on the other, that solitary dissent is triggered by an action, or by the cumulative effect of actions, which catastrophically upsets the balance described by Giddens in structuration theory. Remember that this balance is at once an individual and a social arrangement. For the individual, this catastrophic upset is tantamount to an act of wanton destruction, achieved by steadily disturbing the accepted, recursively implicated distribution of power within that actor's social horizon. This assault is not a sudden *Blitzkrieg* but something more drawn out and 'fifth column'. As long as the individual experiencing mounting concern can continue within the social system as it remains around him or her – as long as the rules and resources keep working and life keeps reproducing itself in broadly similar ways to that which the actor tacitly understands – he or she can avoid the moment when dissent must be expressed. But as soon as one of the central assumptions of the social system in question has been *completely* subverted, then much more than just the personal sensitivities and rules-and-resources conditioning of the individual are placed at risk. Remember that, according to structuration theory, the properties of social systems can be stretched away beyond the control of any one person. Hence, the perception of the risks from such an upset appear much greater to the individual than any personal loss or damage that he or she might now incur by vocalising their dissent[24].

---

[21] Arguably, the most important architect of our time. The Guggenheim Museum in Bilbao is among his works. The Louis Vuitton Foundation building in Paris is another.

[22] An English, 19th century novelist whose prodigious output rested on a very acute observation of the workings of power, class, wealth and poverty, as he observed it. And some of it, particularly the poverty, he observed in Ireland.

[23] One of Trollope's many novels. Part of *The Barsetshire Chronicles*, the book is rich in story-lines that interweave and pull the characters together.

[24] There is a profoundly impressive but appallingly tragic piece of historical writing that exactly describes this steady collapse leading to the solitary voice of dissent –

When something happens, therefore, which brutalises Foucault's *episteme*, something which rocks the structurational arrangement so fundamentally that it begins to topple like a gyro slowing down, the actor cannot avoid a decisive reaction. Continuing with the analogy of the gyroscope, whatever has destroyed his or her certainty[25] is no mere 'precessionary'[26] force to which the cycle of recursive implication can adjust: it will have begun to destabilise *everything* the actor understands. It will be as if a rogue virus has worked its way into the individual's mental software and set about slashing, systematically, at what is found there. Sartre's 'anguish' is no bad way of describing the experience.

Helpfully, we can easily turn this dreadful eruption of emotion into a method for teasing the moment apart. We can actually operationalise it.

The key lies in rules and resources, on the one hand, and their duality and recursive implication, on the other. The method is threefold. First, the reason for dissent exposed by Foucault should be compared with the rules and resources evident in the subject's upbringing and formation, in order to isolate the relevant influences. Second, that refinement needs to be correlated with the subject's career and experience to establish a train of recursive implication – in other words, to confirm that the refined list of relevant influences during upbringing remained valid up to the onset of ontological insecurity. And, third, following Giddens's advice that the rules and resources implicit in this further restatement are in fact a duality and not a dualism, a correlation is then made with the passage of events leading to the act of dissent to establish when duality ceased. At that point, recursive implication was no longer a given and the speed of the subject's personal gyro began to slow down. This matrix should be sufficient for any researcher to take up and apply provided he or she can ac-

---

The World of Yesterday by Stefan Zweig (translated by Anthea Bell). It is essential reading for anyone trying to make sense of the world we have inherited. A second example lies in Rachel Carson's *Silent Spring*, quoted in Chapter 4.

[25] The gyroscope is a useful analogy. Its main property is rigidity in space (in this case 'certainty'). But this is not absolute. The gyro can accept external effects and adjust provided its speed remains constant. If the speed falls then the gyro must topple and its properties are lost.

[26] Precession is a technical term describing the property of a gyro to re-erect itself to a new datum.

cess the innermost self of the subject under investigation. But who knows if you have ever reliably found that?

In the next Chapter, I demonstrate that one can at least come close, even if the subject is yourself.

This Chapter has covered considerable ground and it would be sensible to rehearse its essentials. We began with Foucault and his defence of discontinuity. Slabs of continuity – conventional knowledge – level out that which attempts to disrupt it and even bury discontinuities from sight, purging authorised historical accounts of 'local erudition'. Erudition comprised two distinct strata of knowledge – reasoned, thoughtful knowledge and a messy mix of prejudice and local experience. But even so, despite their subjugation, they retained an insurrectional potential to disrupt the authorised view of how things were. Foucault showed us how 'archaeology' can dig down and release local erudition, effectively by digging a hole as opposed to looking along or across slabs of continuous history.

Next, we learned about discourse and how, by Foucault's reasoning, discursive practices grow with the power within but always remain dependent upon it, while discursive relations which control the outward interface of power can actually accrete their own power and develop an unintended, unauthorised life of their own. The distinction is useful for two reasons. First, it shows us how people and organisations can arrogate power to themselves. And, second, it helps us identify 'domain' or that which is liberated once discursive practices can be separated out: 'domain' or a pure description of discourse at the moment the dissenter speaks out is the context we are looking for. It is upon domain that archaeology can set to work using an insurrection of all those subjugated knowledges that slabs of continuous, convenient thinking have already levelled out.

Then we turned to dissent and, using Giddens, traced its path from ontological insecurity rising within the practical consciousness to a clear articulation of concern expressed through discursive consciousness. Clearly, discursive consciousness follows consciousness of Foucault's domain, which is the link between the two.

We took some time, also, to consider one noteworthy difference between Foucault, whom I called flamboyant, and Giddens whom I described as a novelist. It is a different skillset that we needed now to sift that fine material at the bottom of Foucault's excavated hole – and the sieve was called structuration.

Structuration is concerned with rules (which are constraining) and resources (which are liberating) and the fact, as Giddens insists, that they coexist. They work together. They are not alternatives. Structuration understands, therefore, that the properties of social systems are shaped and perpetuated as we repeat and reinforce those rules and resources which seem relevant over time. We reinforce them in our social lives and through our scope for agency we steadily update, overhaul and husband the structures within which we lead our lives.

The point is that, from this, we can draw down a method – a tool to pick up from that hypothetical workbench which will enable us to get at the precise cause of the growing insecurity and anguish, and explain that crushing responsibility to do something about it. The method rests upon unpicking Giddens's recursive implication right the way back to the rules and resources in the subject's upbringing and then retracing their respective paths through the maturing of the subject's life and experience until evidence of strain and insecurity begins to be apparent. The researcher must follow that growing anguish until the subject can no longer remained silent because the rules and the resources that he or she knows so instinctively are no longer working together.

Chapter 4
Case Study 1 - Martin Kay

My dissent followed mounting concern at the situation of the residents of King's Island, Limerick overheard on BBC radio while out of the country. They had been hit by a major flood on Saturday 1 February 2014. However, my concern was initially a case of self-interest:

> I drove down to King's Island on Monday 3 February 2014 because I had been seen publicly to be identified with the River at Limerick and with River issues and regeneration for at least 18 months (actually about 30 months). The Council had even routed funds in my direction in order that I should be involved in the River. I would have lost credibility completely with the Riverbank audience as well as a number of other quarters, and failed my own personal standards, if I had not taken that immediate step to engage myself with the events on the Island following that week-end.
> (Kay, 2014:51)

My self-interest was soon replaced by a sense of slowly mounting disquiet:

> At first, I simply went shopping for stores needed urgently … or for printing of 'what-to-do' leaflets because no-one knew what to do and no-one would tell them. I even spent €240 from my own pocket to buy sufficient public information leaflets for each of the flood-affected houses because no-one in the public sector or in any charity had bothered to provide them.
> (*ibid.*: 51)

Moral purpose followed:

But I soon became involved in developing a narrative and
record of what occurred because that was the particular skill
I could bring to a situation which had not completely clari-
fied. That skill was called into action because of perceived
failures of response from official quarters. And because people's lives and well-being were at risk – people who had less
than I did by most measures that I could think of – it was
morally imperative for me to respond to that call.
(*ibid.*: 52)

Next, anger fanned the flames of outrage, during the course of six focus
groups:

I remember being appalled at finding a young woman sitting
beside me in the first focus group, and watching her roll up
her sleeves and start showing me the ulcers on her fore-
arms. I have seen such sores in the Third World and I have
even seen them in an off-shore EU island, well south of here
and damned by worse poverty than ours …
"My child has mouth ulcers," she added forcefully and pur-
posefully, "and there's plenty others too."
… but I never thought I would find these sores and ulcers
here in Ireland, in one of our major cities where a Regeneration Agency had enjoyed an annual budget of €5 million for
its own operation, offices, salaries and cars, …
(*ibid.*: 81)

The anger and outrage then became focused through apparent official
indifference:

… the Red Cross had been mounting an appeal for donations in recent days using at least RTE Radio. Donations had
been requested for disaster relief following the flooding –
quite explicitly, for *disaster relief following the flooding*. The
next day, Minister Brian Hayes TD (then, Minister of State
for Public Service Reform and the Office of Public Works)
made a statement on RTE lunchtime radio explaining that

an extra grant had been made to the Irish Red Cross expressly for that purpose. So I contacted the Red Cross that day
[and also the office of Minister Hayes] asking that my message be relayed urgently to their Operations Director and
explaining that a related crisis was developing on King's Island, specifically in St Mary's Park. I said what we were doing and described my role, and then continued:
"... a public health crisis is looming in the two streets named
above. It seems that only people who have a family member
with special needs appear to have been contacted by a public health nurse. Families with known seriously ill members
have not been contacted. No advice has been given on a
household-by-household basis and no house-by-house visits have been made (*sic*). There are now around 50 people, if
not more, *in each of the two streets* named who are showing
signs of infection (mouth ulcers, skin infections, contami-
nated water, and with faeces and rats in the house). And
their situation is getting worse.
"A mobile clinic, whether from the Red Cross or the HSE, is
urgently required on site now with a Public Health specialist
nurse inside it. A trained decontamination team must follow. Furthermore, people who live in the two named streets
need to be told without delay that such a facility is on the
way and that it will arrive by a certain time.
"Please take responsibility for this problem and do not assume that someone else will."
I am grateful to Limerick Regeneration for replying promptly, explaining that HSE policy stood in the way – by which it
meant that HSE policy required people with symptoms to go
to their GP or pharmacy, regardless of context. In other
words, you can be covered in sores and ulcers and be stew-
ing in rats, shit and God-knows-what but you get no special
assistance here. Minister Hayes never said anything by way
of reply and neither did the Red Cross – not then or since ...
(*ibid*.: 81)

It was at this point that my dissent began to crystallise. But I managed to assuage that mounting certainty that something more had to be done, by completing my sequence of focus groups among the flood-affected residents and submitting a detailed report to central and local government: "I would have walked away at that point ... were it not for subsequent developments, all arising without evident explanation from either local or national government, along the Riverbank at King's Island." (*ibid.*: 51). It follows that my dissent was still incomplete.

The intensity of my investigation grew with a sequence of disturbing events over several months – from physical collapses of costly but amateurish flood defences, to the apparent indifference of elected representatives for the area, to oversights and omissions in the drafting of official emergency response plans, to local government's refusal to answer mounting numbers of pressing questions and then, finally, to the revelation that a Major Emergency had never been called in the first place. Two hundred acres, three hundred homes, just thirty minutes to flood the lot – *and no Major Emergency called.*

It also became apparent, after my dissent had formed, that spontaneous donations of financial aid, given at the time of the flood to assist the residents affected, still remained in various bank accounts 11 months later and had not been passed on. Furthermore, it emerged that upstream Ardnacrusha Power Station had discharged more than 32 million tonnes of turbine water into the swollen river in the 24 hours before the flood arrived, and the same amount in the 24 hours after. At the time of the flood, however, the strong impression circulated, apparently from official sources, was that the Power Station had not discharged anything at all.

The final straw, so it seemed, was the conclusion that powerful interests, organising the year-long 'Limerick City of Culture' celebration, did not want the publicity of a Major Emergency on their doorstep – and a more effective, efficient and formal response to the plight of the flood-affected residents was duly sacrificed. The 'discontinuity' presented by the King's Islanders was removed from the official view of local history. By that point, I was well and truly dissenting, and voiced my own 'discontinuity' in turn:

Can you see how 'corrosive', as I put it earlier, questionable administration, disorganisation and doubtful leadership can be? As the rot becomes clearer, it leads someone who is try-

ing to analyse a given context for entirely valid purposes into ever tightening circles of disbelief and ultimately rejection of the public position, whatever that might be and whatever it might allege. I was sufficiently unimpressed at what I discovered that I realise that I, too, was approaching that same sense of disaffection I detected and reported to An Taoiseach[27] in February – by which I mean alienation from, and ill-disposition towards, local governance and officialdom. Guidance Note 11, *central government's own advice*, even warns expressly that disaffection is what happens in these circumstances. And, in my case, I had reached that state because I could deduce only that the system of local governance was sloppy and attentive to itself, when it should have been effective and attentive to those the system was meant to serve. Poor people on the outside merited, in the system's scheme of things, no attention at all – and both sides knew it.
(*ibid.*: 118)

I explained at the outset of that book what I was going to do:

I have put my 'journey' down on paper in this way to help other people think in advance about the adequacy of preparations where they live and about their own vulnerability, and I have tried to do it in a way that will shock them wherever I was shocked. This is because what I discovered is disquieting – and if I once lose that sense of disbelief and disquiet, then we will all conveniently forget about the deep dismay that followed.
(*ibid.*: 6)

Disquiet, disbelief and deep dismay. Self-interest, moral purpose, anger, slowly mounting outrage, and ultimately rejection. The crescendo is easily discerned and some guess may reasonably be made, as a conse-

---

[27] The name in the Irish language for the Prime Minister of Ireland.

quence, at the seams in the rock under my feet. For example, something to do with 'honour'; standards instilled through earlier professional training and experience; an innate sense of social justice; an ideal view of public service; and a determination to see things through once involvement had started. The tenacity evident in the latter may in truth have started in an otherwise empty in-tray but other aspects may well have been 'genetically' induced. For example, I can hear one, if not both, of my parents saying, *in extremis*, "How dare you …!" and "How dare they …!" (I have since learned that other parents may not have routinely reacted in this way.)

However, there was also the 'backcloth' provided by the concepts I chose to distil from the events laid out in the book. These included social decay, an absence of accountability, and, apparently, the real cause of my dissent: "I am comfortable … in identifying this Darkness I have been talking about as the *hegemonic tendencies* of public governance here …" (*ibid.*: 142, italics added). Put bluntly, I don't like the calculating indifference and threatening, oafish control of thoughtless repetition and, dare I say it, of incompetents and of bullies: none had any place in my professional upbringing[28] whence all that failed to make the grade were ruthlessly purged.

But there were other influences – and they are not completely straightforward.

First, there was that original, strong sense of even-handedness which surfaced again later: "… it is something to do with me being able to look in the mirror as well as being prepared to hold it up to others." (*ibid.*: 149) This is more significant than it may appear. I can recall another instance, 16 years earlier, when I had stood up and walked out of a semi-State Board Meeting (effectively showing my dissent). I did this because I did not recognise the truth of what was being said by a certain (executive) Member of the Board. I suppose a cannier operator would have said nothing and then played his or her cards accordingly. But I did not have any cards to play,

---

[28] In my first career, I was a naval officer, maritime helicopter pilot and, eventually, squadron commander. We could not afford incompetence or inefficiency. Our lives depended on the best qualities and the best performance … And as I write the preceding sentence, I suddenly recall that not only my father but also each male on the maternal side of my family, for at least 200 years, went to sea and survived that same, unforgiving experience. As they say in Ireland: "It wasn't off the ground I licked it."

being only a contracted adviser and not a Board Member (either executive or non-executive). I could only remove myself from something concealed and, to me, dishonourable – and all the Board Members noticed. I suppose, therefore, that in that earlier instance I was concerned for whatever I might have understood that my own integrity comprised, even at the risk to my professional contract. And some similar instinct arose again at the time of the Limerick flood. By 'being able to look in the mirror', then, I am saying that these were my moments of liberation.

Second, my 'uncanniness' in the incident reported above may be related to the fact that I had very recently lost my partner to cancer – a very sad and protracted decline, in the care and management of which I was intimately involved. And in the later case of 'being able to look in the mirror', I had then also recently attended my father's prolonged deathbed. So life-changing events, like grief and pity, may also impact considerably upon the senses sufficiently as to pare away the capacity for tolerating and absorbing reasons to dissent[29]. Case Study 4 reinforces the point.

And third, there was an influence I did not put in the book but am obliged to declare here. I regretted the fact that, despite my involvement in river affairs and my considerable experience in matters relating to the context of the flood, I had been unable to secure any formally employed position in my area of activity and in that place. The need for such expertise was evident but no job was ever offered, despite the reasonable suspicion that 'jobs for the boys' were being created not far, in organisational terms, from where I was giving my services for an occasional cheque to offset expenses (*ibid.*: 110). My consciousness reasoned that had I been employed to work in those same areas, where officialdom was content for me to labour with only the odd contribution to my costs, the official response to the flooding of King's Island would have been 'a damn sight more effective' than it had proved. And then there was also the affront from officialdom, in that my involvement with the flood-affected residents had caused a certain personality to instruct me to remove myself from that same river regeneration programme that I had designed and in which official quarters had a nominal interest (*ibid.*: 96). Again put bluntly, there

---

[29] For completeness, I should report that I did not take bereavement counselling in either case despite being advised to do so after the earlier death. This omission on my part may well have accentuated the emotions which clouded my double experience of dissent.

were some who did not like it that people from the poorest parts of town, who were not part of the 'City of Culture' and therefore did not 'matter' in the greater scheme of things, were being helped to raise their profile. *Their distress was inconvenient to those who needed no inconvenience.* And so they took it out on me – and I may have reacted, in turn, against them.

A clash of emotions on both sides leading to mutual resentment, therefore, can also come into this complex mix. And perhaps resentment, at that moment in time, was also sharpened by the simultaneous sense of loss identified above.

I am surprised that I have divulged so much – and struck, also, by the resonance between the way my anger mounted and that seen in perhaps the greatest work of environmental dissent ever, Rachel Carson's *Silent Spring* (2000). This book exposes the destructive impact of pesticides upon wildlife (hence, a spring without birdsong). As the environmental historian and biographer, Linda Lear, put it in her 'Afterword' to that reprint of Carson's mid-20th century research: "Carson became bolder and angrier as she gathered her research" (*ibid.*: 258).

I had not understood, either, that there was so much to uncover and dig out. But that, of course, was without the assistance of Michel Foucault. And having written the preceding paragraphs with sincerity and the serious objective of capturing as much as I possibly could from the circumstances of the flood and from my own conscious memory, I turned to genealogy and discourse.

The latter can be dealt with fairly quickly. There was a discourse of 'regeneration' through which Council effort and services were channelled. And its participants, who were charged with managing the recovery from the flood in addition to the everyday business of local government, did not like it that I had cut across their 'patch' rather than run with its grain. They particularly did not like it when I began to ask questions and 'hold up a mirror' to what had not been done, hence my ordered removal from riverside regeneration activities. It was this same discourse that had generated occasional contributions to my costs and, therefore, may have thought me disloyal, something to be punished or at least removed and smoothed over. The externalities, moreover – the discursive relations of the regeneration discourse who were now preparing to bid for *City of Culture 2020* – did not need the bad news of a first anniversary of the flood: their power was growing and, from a sequence of overtly positive reports in *The Limerick Leader*[30] anything critical was 'subjugated' in favour of the preferred story-line.

I turned next to genealogy. Quite deliberately, I turned away from my emotions, from my recollection of recent events and from my perception of a 'regeneration discourse', towards the idea of an 'insurrection of knowledges'. And I was surprised that something very obvious had escaped me, and would have continued to escape me, if I had not first begun to think in terms of 'subjugated knowledge'.

King's Island, Limerick, which is shaped like a flint axe-head with the slightly broader end to the north and the base to the south, is bounded by the River Shannon on the western side and the Abbey River on the eastern and southern sides. In the years immediately following the declaration of the Free State (in 1922), a number of river fishermen, known collectively as 'the Abbey Fishermen', progressively bought out the riparian fishing rights in that area of both the Abbey and the Shannon. Hitherto, these rights would have been the exclusive preserve of the 'gentry' and the 'ascendancy'. But those who bought them out were very ordinary Irishmen of no great formal education, acting collectively. Perhaps because they daily faced the dangers of the most dangerous river in Ireland (*ibid.*: 13 *et seq.*), these men were characterised by epic humanity: the Abbey fishermen gave the right to fish (by daylight) to any local man who had no other means of feeding his family. Compared with the preceding centuries of exclusion, suppression and enforced poverty, this was an unprecedented act of kindness and solidarity. When the Ardnacrusha power station was built in the 1930s, however, together with its lethal salmon traps at the purposely designed Thomond Weir, the Electricity Supply Board bought out compulsorily the rights of the Abbey Fishermen. Not only did this allow the ESB to kill most of the hibernating salmon for huge, unprecedented profit (right on the doorstep of the Abbey Fishermen, incidentally) but it drove the local men, who could not otherwise feed their families, into illegality.

I had become involved with this story in the course of conducting an oral history programme among the people of the river bank at Limerick. In

---

[30] Particularly in mid-March 2015 after the damaging revelation (7 March) that the new Council was in a state of total chaos.

2012, I wrote a short 'pen-picture' based upon that sequence of testimonies in order that I could summarise the local history for a wider audience without compromising my ethical undertakings to those I had interviewed. The pen-picture is repeated below in full, in order to convey the historical nature of the 'ground below the feet' of the Abbey Fishermen. The few sentences referring to those same men are italicised, in order to emphasise what a very small part of that particular investigation this trace of a 'subjugated knowledge' actually constituted:

> Along the main street of the Island, children were running and calling, backwards and forwards between the houses on each side, dashing in and out on errands and messages, and playing ritually with chalk, stones and make-believe. Women were talking on the doorstep, keeping the bonds of local knowledge alive, sharing news with those who need to know and resources with those they know in need. Some women were still children, grown up before their time.
>
> *Down towards the River, just yards away, men are queuing up to cast their lines into the water. Bamboo sticks ripple along the bridges and the waterfront, some alive and lethal with eel fry, some aloft just waiting their turn. Behind them, others are working on boats, ropes and fishing lines, inspecting nets and assembling hemp for the Island's net-maker,* a woman called Chrissie Benn, known still in local legend for her lame leg and talented fingers. *Some men only come out at night – in boats, on steps and along ledges – alert, like all hunters, from the moment they leave home. Silently, half-men accompany them, just children learning a trade, but not half-paid.* The women stayed at home and triumphed in their own ways.
>
> Out of sight, within the yard, nets grow steadily, strung from the ancient hooks set in the wall, as gentle fists tie knots and bends, deftly expert like all sea-people but these, being women, never sailing far from home. Those, who can, buy-in their nets. Fishing debris steadily accumulates. Stones like

dumb-bells. Corks and floats, nets and lines. Paddles of different sizes. Memories, too, big ones and little ones.

For up the River, a new tradition has died – perhaps the greatest democracy the Shannon has ever known yet cut off in one abrupt, un-republican stroke when the new power station at Ardnacrusha began to take control. Undeterred but deeply wounded, the Abbey men today still honour this history and strengthen their own legends by paddling back and back again, by subterfuge still taking fish, and by following in the ways they had always set out.

Below, the River is different. Some men went that way instead – seen, perhaps, like invading Norsemen but this time coming out with the tide and with new techniques and outboard engines. Coonagh men from the estuary will tell us all in time. And someone will tell us, too, how the River can bind all its people together and yet still seem different if I stand just here and look there, compared with standing there and looking here …

… which is why there was always the other island, St. Thomas Island[31], where people summered, swam and socialised – and the week-end life in the Athlunkard club where men and women mingled, because it was a proper house and not a shed where boats were built. Together again at the end of each week, they played and picnicked up the Abbey on family excursions free of fish but still afloat. Always afloat. For they were River people and the River ran in their veins.

At the start of the new week and back in Nicholas Street, the ancient centre of the City, life rolled on continuously. Men

---

[31] St. Thomas Island lies just north of King's Island beside the 'tail race' leading towards Ardnacrusha Power Station. The Island is a 'palimpsest' of historical remains and civilisation – but for the Islanders a generation ago, it was literally like Ballybunion. And for those from other countries, Ballybunion was like Blackpool or Staten Island. It was just that the Islanders hadn't the money or the means to get to such exotic places: they could only walk and swim, or row their boats, to St. Thomas Island.

and boys would criss-cross the bustle and renewed gossip to deliver the hemp for Chrissie Benn and bring the new nets back to the side of the boats. Women would come along the street each morning with fresh-caught fish to sell down in the Docks. A Cusack[32] making nets here while a Cusack bought the fish there. Somewhere, a neighbour would be off on his bicycle, collecting the insurance as the clocks ticked on and children filed inside their separate classroom doors – while O'Farrells and McNamaras, Clancys, Quinlivans and many more, kept their heritage alive by still working the River in their boats and bringing, still, the catch home to their families in spite of the new State's gross officialdom. The names alone entangled them. Everything else was survival and simplicity.

The penultimate line in the quote above contains the phrase "the new State's gross officialdom". The pen-picture in which it was contained was inserted on the first page of the opening chapter of my book, my statement of dissent, about the Limerick flood (*ibid.*: 13). I very quickly realised, however, that, on nearly the last page of that same book, I had included another example of gross officialdom (*ibid.*: 163) emanating from essentially the same source. This took the form of an announcement from the Limerick City and County Council of a new flood management arrangement for St Mary's (the main flooded part of King's Island and, incidentally, that part of the city with which many Abbey fishermen would have been identified).

My first of a number of serious difficulties with the Council's announcement was that there was no place reserved in this arrangement for the people of St Mary's, among whom lay greater river-knowledge than anyone in the Council. In other words, not even three quarters of an intervening century had served to overthrow the gross officialdom of the State and replace it with something more inclusive and receptive to local experience and erudition. I had even complained, in a contemporaneous letter

---

[32] Chrissie Benn was also a Cusack. The man who bought the fish was René Cusack, from quite a different family.

to the local newspaper in 2014, in response to the Council's announcement, that a committee of local residents had yet again been ignored: "... grass roots democratic representation has no value in this city" (*ibid.*: 125).

Suddenly, my dissent seemed even more nuanced than I had earlier imagined, when working solely with my personal feelings and recollections – for, evidently, the 'ground under the feet' of the Abbey Fishermen and the King's Islanders had, to some extent, become the ground under my own feet, too. Simultaneously, Foucault's sometimes cranky, certainly obscure but always entertainingly idiosyncratic theorising of genealogy and discourse had become super-relevant to what I was trying to understand[33].

Only one thing seemed absolutely clear to me. If any single instance or event had 'authored' my dissent, and kept me on my feet when others had gone, it had been manufactured by other people.

We said earlier that 'domain' is discourse stripped of its discursive trail, the pure description of the facts of the discourse at that point in time. The externalities, the discursive relations, might form part of this domain but the discursive practices did not. And, next, that something in that domain gives rise to the actor's dissent.

In my experience, it was the persistence of gross officialdom *and still at the expense of the same poor people* that caused my dissent: gross officialdom furthermore, was inconsistent with the democracy that was meant to underpin the situation[34]. The cause of my dissent lay broadly within 'the State', in agencies as diverse as the City/County Council, central government departments and leading national charities. The cause was scattered but became focused with the linkage of a severe flood which impacted upon an identifiable group of people and area with both of

---

[33] I already knew from my own Ph.D. research (Kay, 2009) that Foucault's teaching on discourse, the second of my investigative tools in this paper, could be reliably observed reproduced in society generally and at the interface with the State specifically.

[34] It is interesting to note that, in the *Irish Examiner*, 14 April 2015, the elected Members of Limerick City and County Council are reportedly "furious at being literally fobbed off by officialdom at Limerick City Hall" (p. 7). Clearly, others agreed with me.

which I had had considerable involvement. My involvement had even become personal and intimate: I had conducted oral history there, I had immersed myself in the river-bank (but not literally). I had stood in front of the flood-affected residents in all their tears and distress. And I had told them "I care enough to listen to what you are trying to tell us".

Without Foucault's clarifying effect, the casual reader might have been content to conclude that a mix of unremarkable, unconnected factors, things we don't need much to bother about, lay beneath it all.

There remained, however, a proxy character to my anguish: I was never brought up on the riverbank at Limerick; I wasn't even born in Ireland; I was a 'blow-in', there by invitation and acceptance only. Why had the ground under my feet merged with the ground around the Island Path? Why was I standing up when others, who were much more closely implicated in Limerick's history and might have stood up, had not?

My belief that structuration theory provided a method for answering that question required me to:

1. Identify the 'un-seived' reasons for dissent as unearthed by Foucault.

2. Compare them with the rules and resources in my upbringing and formation in order to isolate the relevant ones.

3. Correlate the relevant influences with my developing carer and experience in order to confirm a pattern of recursive implication.

4. And then look for the point where my sense of comfort began to creak – the point at which ontological insecurity began to manifest itself.

5. Finally, I needed to track the duality of the refined and implicated rules and resources to the point where duality could no longer be assured. At that point, I would find myself impelled to stand up and fulfil my 'crushing responsibility' to say "No!" and to commit to that declaration. My hypothetical gyro would by then have toppled irrecoverably.

My broad conclusions, before turning to Foucault's genealogy to refine the rough chunks unearthed by archaeological excavation, had been that my dissent had been caused by: revulsion at the hegemonic tendencies of local governance; a need to demonstrate my own integrity while criticising that of others ("being able to look in the mirror ..." etc); the coincidence of personal bereavement leading to a redirection of pity and concern; and resentment that my own experience had been overlooked and that poor people did not seem to matter. With the benefit of genealogy, I was able to restate it as the subjugation of local knowledges, both in the 1930s and *again* at the end of 2014. Clearly, what I ended up with was not what I started with.

I then began to scour my early memories to discover where this conclusion might resonate with the rules and resources that affected me then.

In contrast with both my parents, I did not have a settled upbringing but have lived in an excessive number of places that I called 'home' and participated in an excessive number of educational systems and circumstances: I am embarrassed to admit how many. But I would go further and say that I have no sense of origin beyond one. Although my parents were white and privileged, I was borne in a Tamil region of (then) Ceylon in an area that has since been decimated by jungle, civil war, genocide and finally tsunami. I learned somewhere that the house we lived in does not even exist anymore. The particular memory that resonates in me still is that the knowledge of the Tamil culture, which was the real heir to the coastlines of Ceylon, was ruthlessly and cruelly effaced over time. Furthermore, Tamil marginalisation originated in the gross officialdom of British colonial diplomacy which, I believe, chose the wrong side when it came to Celanese Independence. Even the staff in our own house did not like the one Tamil 'house-boy' (which was how he was referred to) who was very dear to me[35].

If there was any stability in my upbringing (in other words, recursive implication of rules and resources) from Ceylon onwards, it was that the maritime tradition was everywhere around me. Our home was even by the sea. Furthermore, every male forebear on my mother's distaff side had gone to sea for over 200 years - sailing slave ships, warships and famine ships – and I had even spent 19 years at sea myself. My father himself had served at sea and built his career in maritime economy, audit and administration. The sea, its culture and its language were everywhere: my playthings included an old Seaman's Knife, with Marlin Spike, and a Bosun's Call; and I remember that we even called the toilet 'the heads' and reproduced other naval terminology unthinkingly around the house. But the real point about the sea, that infused every aspect of my youth and experience, was that it is an unforgiving environment requiring discipline, prac-

---

[35] His name was Banda and I record it her by way of redress for the insult of being described as a house-boy.

tice, mutual respect, honesty and integrity. My father's career was built on such standards – and it was his career which we followed and his standards which we replicated. That was my formative environment.

To me, those rules and resources encapsulated all that was relevant and essential, which in turn continued to be refreshed and re-endorsed as my own career, as a maritime aviator and, for 19 years, a sea-going officer unfolded. Within that time, I had direct experience of Search & Rescue and of disaster relief. In other words, I knew what had to be done when people were engulfed in sea-water out of control or damaged by some other maritime eventuality. Unsurprisingly, I found it hard when the time came to leave the sea to adapt to the slower, more relaxed pace of civilian life where people generally lived dry, comfortable and unexposed lives. It was only when I became involved with the people of the riverbank at Limerick – 65 nautical miles inland but still, unusually, a tidal and, therefore, a 'coastal' city – that I rediscovered that same sense of respect for the water and of familiarity with what could and could not be safely undertaken upon it. Small wonder that the ground under their feet soon became mine. And it was something of a relief at last to be rooted somewhere with which I could sympathise and which sympathised in turn with me. This suggested that I had never completely turned away from the water: I had neglected other opportunities and only ever recursively implicated in my developing social life that which I sorely missed. In effect, when I became involved with King's Island and the riverbank at Limerick, and because there was no Tamil home to turn to, or anywhere else for that matter, I had 'come home'[36].

My ontological insecurity began to creak about one year before the flooding of King's Island, specifically when I began to realise that the City Council had not the slightest interest in the River Shannon except in so far as it impinged upon their plans for *Limerick City of Culture 2020*. There is a parallel there with the Tamil experience at the time of Ceylon's Independence. Such indifference to the power of the water was professional anathema to me. Just as bad, official indifference to the deteriorating state

---

[36] This also resonated with my maternal grandfather's experience. He had no home and started life on the docks in Liverpool, orphaned at the age of 4 years, I understand, by one of the great influenza epidemics of the 1870s. Following his first unhappy voyage from Ireland, he eventually returned to the sea where he made his home in the British Navy's Royal Marines.

of the riverbank was facilitating the spread of dangerous invasive species. Even worse, it was aggravating the risk of flooding through the consequent degradation of the riverbanks. My sense of background anxiety continued to grow and I felt bound to campaign publicly about it using a blog that became well respected (www.voiceoftheriver.net) The blog lasted over a year but I was later instructed to close it down. Such an instruction is typical of the well-understood reactions of hegemony once challenged – namely to reassert control by whatever means are available to it.

You can see, can't you, that I was heading for an outburst, although I was still able to carry on in a state of non-dissent or acquiescence. I even carried on through the days immediately following the flood when I imagined that the conspicuously absent best-practice responses to serious flooding would soon be restored and that my sense of greater calm would similarly return.

I found, however, that the duality of what I could accomplish or replicate with respect to the river at Limerick, in terms of safety, awareness, management, good husbandry, education and so on, suddenly failed within the month after the flooding of King's Island. The actual moment was finished, my gyro had completely toppled, when no-one – *no-one* – responded to that essential reaction in disaster relief which is to provide on-site relief and medical aid. To be sure, volunteers provided food, stores and blankets but the authorities, national and local, did not bat an eyelid about the desperate state the poorest people in Limerick found themselves in. And the moment of my dissent had started in that third quote in this Chapter, where I refer to 'failures of response from official quarters'. It is interesting to note that that third quote was associated in the forgoing text with 'moral purpose' (a phrase I wrote very early on in drafting and have not changed since). Significantly, I think, this confirms for me the relevance of the teaching of Jean-Paul Sartre: anguish leading to a crushing responsibility to do something about it.

This conclusion was close to the point that Foucault took me but only Giddens helped me pin it down. Everything that followed was consolidation of my dissent.

Chapter 5

Case Study 2 - Fr Tony Flannery

Fr Flannery's early training lay in the harsh Redemptorist discipline of denial of the self and submission to the (Redemptorist) Superior "as the will of God" (Flannery, 2013: 13). And yet, in his young days, this iron teaching underwent a sudden, fundamental shift with a contradictory, new and utterly consuming vision articulated through Vatican II: "The glory of God is the human person fully alive" (*ibid*.: 15, citing St Irenaeus). This meant in practice that: "[the] days of telling people what to do were gone ..." (*ibid*.: 18).

It is important to note that Flannery took the decision to accept ordination *after* this exciting change. In fact, he was on the points of leaving the congregation before that shift in vision took place.

Flannery enjoyed his mission, his role and his purpose. He went about his work with balance and energy. And yet a sense of unease was soon growing within him:

> I could see very clearly how the Church was losing touch with young people, how its [uncompromising] language and style of communication were no longer getting through to them ...
> Many a time I came home from a day in school wondering what was the point of it all ...
> (*ibid*.: 20)

And, eventually he began to speak openly (often when preaching) about the difficulties within the Church: "There was too much that was dysfunctional about the Church and Vatican that needed to be voiced" (*ibid*.: 22). Next, he wrote about it in miscellaneous articles, followed by regular opinions and, then, in a succession of books:

There were a number of controversial parts in [the second book] but it did not draw the ire of the Vatican; nor did a [third] book ... During these years I also wrote a regular monthly column for the Redemptorist publication *Reality*. (*ibid.*: 25)

Flannery was actively and extensively speaking from his conscience about matters of conviction and about "an institution that was falling apart" (*ibid.*: 27) in the wake of the scandal of child sex abuse. To his objection to retrenchment from the enlightenment of Vatican II could now be added the outrage that some clerics were involved in "unspeakable crimes", but not being called to account. The former was a question of theology and ministry, but latter was a question of culpability, of moral and legal failure:

... a sense of shame and horror at what some of our colleagues had done, as well as anger at bishops and religious superiors for their failure to act promptly and decisively. [Flannery and his contemporary parish priests] felt a sense of utter frustration with the Vatican, because Church leaders consistently refused to look at the deeper questions raised ...

(*ibid.*: 27)

To shock at the Vatican's mishandling of clerical sex abuse was soon added disappointment that the related question of clerical celibacy was not on the agenda, and at the increasingly centralised power structure of the Church. Part of the problem lay in 'congregations' – discrete power structures that dealt with different aspects of the government of the Church. Eventually:

... the Congregation for the Doctrine of the Faith (CDF) assumed more and more control over the whole Church and instead of being a servant of decision makers, actually became a decision maker itself ...

It is remarkable how closely, in this short sentence, Flannery is unknowingly following Foucault's explanation of the way that discursive relations feed off the power within. He continues:

... [This] was an unhealthy development. The hopes arising from the Second Vatican Council, of a new style of govern-ance based on collegiality, were trampled upon; instead we seemed to be heading back to a 19th century model of Church. Meanwhile, in Ireland we had bishops who, while good and sincere in themselves, seemed to possess no real leadership ability, never venturing in public an opinion that in any way challenged the *diktat* of Rome.
(*ibid.*: 28)

In 2010, with seven colleagues, and three months later with 300 priests, Flannery formed The Association of Catholic Priests (ACP) which would speak out for the renewal of the Church in line with the vision of Vatican II and provide a voice for parish priests. But this was *collective* dissent, ex-actly as Arendt envisaged it, and not his solitary voice. That came later.

Before long, Flannery felt the wrath of the CDF. After a year as one of the leaders of the ACP, Flannery was called to a meeting with his superior. He was not allowed in advance to know the content of this meeting (an ominous event in any profession). Next, he was telephoned from Rome (hitherto unheard of) and was told that he was in serious trouble: "I got a sick feeling in the pit of my stomach" (*ibid.*: 35) and not unnaturally, but arguably unfortunately, told his host and circle of friends what had just happened:

... the CDF got extremely angry when my case was made public later. I believe that their concern is not likely to have anything to do with the good name of the priest [as the CDF had insisted] but rather with their obsession with keeping their own archaic and unjust practices from being aired in public.
(*ibid.*:37)

It is at this point that the eventual object of Flannery's solitary, as op-posed to collective, dissent becomes clear:

It is one thing to read about this type of thing happening to other people. But when it comes bursting into your own life it is very unsettling. (*ibid.*:37)

Flannery elaborates his ontological insecurity with absolute clarity. It is remarkably consistent with Giddens's earlier explanation of the failure in the crisis of self-identity and the failure in the constancy of the individual's social and material environment:

> We draw much of our security from our belief that we have our lives under control, from our knowledge of what we will be doing into the future. We hope that we will be able to continue in a meaningful occupation and weather any uncertainty that might come along the way. When something happens that puts all these plans in jeopardy one is left a bit like a boat on the ocean after the engines cut off. What is this going to do to my future? Will I be able to cope? Can my health survive the stress and pressure that are certain to accompany this?
> (*ibid.*:38)

This being ontological insecurity, however, it follows that Flannery was still not yet actually dissenting. His separate crescendo of *solitary* concern had not yet started. As he prepares for his visit to Rome, however, he talks of the "inhumanity of the processes engaged in by the Vatican" (*ibid.*: 41); and on arrival, of repeated warnings "in no uncertain terms" of the gravity of his situation (*ibid.*: 42). This brow-beating was followed by his confusion and uncertainty at being presented with a relatively innocent list of quotes drawn from his articles[37] – and then the unexpected 'block-buster' of a harsh, un-Christian-like[38] judgement from "a hard rigid system that imposed rules and exercised old-style control" (*ibid.*: 51). By now, Flannery was angry that his withdrawal from everything his ministry stood for and his suspension from every activity he had pursued in the spirit of the Vatican II, was being ordered by a body which had demonstrably cut across the teaching of Vatican II and plunged the Church, *his* Church, back into 'the dark ages'.

---

[37] Is there not an echo here of the black art and psychology of the torturer? I have read something, somewhere. If any knows where, I do not need to be told.

[38] The term 'un-Christian-like' is the author's, not Fr Flannery's.

It is this sudden evidence of perversion of the teaching of the Church, tantamount to treachery, that led to Flannery's solitary dissent. And we can only guess at the instant impact it had upon his sense of well-being:

Even now as I edit this book, reading through the pages of diktats makes me angry again! I was lucky that I had my brother with me to support me at the meeting.
(*ibid*.:51)

At this same point in time, Flannery was even "in the mood for confrontation" (*ibid*.: 63), although a vein of practical thinking, led by his brother, Frank, did achieve a calming of the situation and a way out of the meeting. However, Flannery had not yet declared his dissent beyond explaining, first, that he did not think he would be able to comply with the *sentire cum Ecclesia*[39] as the Vatican required, following a suitable period of reflection; and, second, that he declined to stand down from his leadership role in ACP. This quality of 'barter' can be explained by Flannery's recognition that the real power was not in the room – in other words, his interlocutor in Rome was something of a messenger and the message would be delivered later. Even on return to Ireland, his "anger with the Vatican persisted" but, he reminded himself "he was willing to go along with the process as agreed" (*ibid*.: 69). So, his dissent still remained private (as required by the Vatican), even though colleagues and companions knew that all was not well.

But, suddenly, the news did break – and with it, examples of other instances of enforced silence and censorship. But Flannery still went along with his various undertakings given in Rome, with the exception of involvement in the ACP. Before long, however, events conspired that the ACP achieved a significant media status in Ireland and "a far greater position of influence than the Catholic hierarchy" (*ibid*.: 79). This was not what the Vatican expected. Rome responded with an anonymous accusation of heresy and the threat of excommunication (*ibid*.: 82). At a further meeting in Rome, the survival of the career of Flannery's Superior was leveraged against him: "You might think that you are the person most under pressure here. But you are not" (*ibid*.: 85). In effect, they were all of

---

[39] The order, literally, to think with the Church - in other words, to tow the party line.

them in a murky suspension of medieval terror that only Flannery could resolve.

With the imminent pressure of the Eucharistic Congress (to be held in Ireland in June 2012), Flannery was increasingly urged to release the required statement[40], about which he prevaricated – although a draft offered by Flannery was later agreed by the CDF. But then retirements came and personalities changed in Rome. There was a brief lull and then a new Cardinal took over. New instructions followed, which were even harsher than before, and further reflection was ordered: "The upshot of these instructions was that I was to be definitely silenced and removed from ministry" (*ibid.*: 98). And at this point, Flannery lost his patience: he considered that he was being bullied and, by the inclusion of new instructions on wider issues, that a trap was being laid.

In his written response to a document containing instructions sent from Rome, in September 2012, Flannery published his position in full. Interestingly, Flannery spoke from the perspective of Vatican II, whereas the instructions he was responding to were written from the perspective of the new leadership of the CDF (which, emphatically, was not that of Vatican II). It must have seemed to Flannery that he was declaring 'Check mate!' Certainly, his response was "a very different offering" from that expected (*ibid.*: 121) and was, constructively, his declaration of solitary dissent from the power and methods of the CDF.

As a consequence, he next received the "nuclear warhead" equivalent of a formal precept of obedience (*ibid.*: 123) – something quite separate from the core belief of the Church expressed through Vatican II, something that the CDF could exploit. This concerned a forthcoming meeting of the ACP. Flannery was not, under any circumstances, to attend and he was required furthermore to give such an undertaking without delay. Not only did Flannery refuse but he examined his conscience carefully to understand why he should refuse. And then he published his book explaining every twist and turn, his moral unease, and his perception of a growing gulf between the CDF and the valid and authentic teaching of his Church, namely that of Vatican II. His is a narrative of extreme courage and extreme moral certainty.

---

[40] This would confirm the error of his ways and his intention, henceforth, to conform with current teaching.

So, how can Foucault help us further?

Flannery himself has already explained how the CDF was a startling instance of discursive relations accreting power when "… instead of being a servant of decision makers, [it] actually became a decision maker itself …" It seems reasonable, therefore, to remain with discourse.

Some 10 or 12 years before this book was written, a telephone conversation on RTE Radio 1's *Liveline* included the chance remark from one lady caller: "We had a religion but what we got was a Church" (or words to that effect). In that short sentence, it is possible to glimpse how power starts and practices grow: it all began with faith but ended up in organisation.

We are taught that the beginnings of the Christian faith derive from the Acts of the Apostles and that the Church moved outwards as the 'good news' spread. St Paul led the advance, from Jerusalem to Rome, and developed the message in his various Letters. By Foucault's reasoning, that was the power within: Christ lit it, St Paul fanned it and, by the power of the Holy Spirit, the faith spread. If the first practice of the Church had been Baptism and the second encapsulated in the Last Supper, the third and final practice was that the message of 'Christ crucified' was symbolised in the Cross. Notwithstanding, Constantine ruthlessly developed Christianity into a vast bureaucratic machine and the Christianisation of Europe – with all its discontinuities, machinations, secrecy, declarations of heresy, and ultimately violence and bloodshed – had begun. A discourse of normalisation had long since developed and, with it, structures of immense power and wealth.

It was not the original faith that lost its way but the work of men that distorted things: discursive practices which not all could support; the arrogation of power to themselves by discursive relations; and the ultimate arrival of Renaissance and all that followed Enlightenment.

Small wonder that Flannery was excited by Vatican II, after centuries of conservatism, and persuaded to stay and accept ordination. That particular experience was power/knowledge of a beneficial sort, whereas the subsequent reversal of the message of Vatican II was altogether darker. This was the work of discursive relations, organisations which feed off the power within and grow their own power in turn. The CDF is the prime example. Earlier, through the period after Vatican I, the power within did probably stay unchanged but the discursive practices that had drawn their power from it over centuries past began to look steadily more and more old-fashioned and out of date. Those authoritarian practices died hard and found eventual relief and revival in the reversal of the impact of Vatican II. The innate conservatism of the Church, as discursive practice, had nursed them through some barren years while religious dissent and nonconformism appeared to thrive outside the Church.

But then, what appeared to be a taking-back of the Church's practices to centuries past was actually the forward vision of the supreme discursive relation, the CDF. Meanwhile, the pitiable, higher levels of the Redemptorist Order who attempted to mediate between Flannery and the CDF were lost in a time-warp of muddle, uncertainty and confused understanding of how things ought now to be done. Traditionally, the Redemptorists had been keepers of the hard-line but now a greater authority had replaced them, and its anonymous representatives were breathing very heavily down a number of evidently frightened Superior necks.

"Farewell to reason!" says Flyvbjerg, speaking of the situation in Aalborg – but just as relevantly of the situation the Redemptorist Order was experiencing:

… the less power an actor has, the more emphasis is placed on reason; and the more power, the less weight. Reason is one of the few forms of power that those without much influence still possess.
(1998: 132)

And repeated Redemptorist appeals to reason failed where Fr Flannery was concerned. A different discourse now prevailed and, for Flannery, that discourse had cut across the beauty, the simplicity, the humility and the Christian validity of the message of Vatican II, *the one thing that made him stay and devote his life to ministry*. And the way the power of the CDF had accomplished this had made him very, very angry.

Let us now consider, therefore, the question of subjugated knowledges. The first act of subjugation lies in the concerted reversal of Vatican II. The subsequent act, for the purposes of this book, lies in the attempt to suppress what Flannery had been saying in his articles and books[41]. The

---

[41] We might say that the exclusion of questions of reform, for example, clerical celibacy, from the agenda were also acts of subjugation.

discourse of the Church, in the direction its discursive practices were now being guided, sought to replace that 'heresy'. (Flannery himself talks of the secretive way in which the Vatican set about this work, a gross error of management, it might be claimed, which the wise manager or administrator would be ill-advised to replicate today: do not try and suppress such knowledges but find a way in which they can be aired, shared and calmly managed.)

Consider, therefore, the insurrection which followed Flannery's ontological insecurity and growing concern. He and others who shared his concern channelled their efforts through the ACP which actually achieved, at the level of Parish Priest, a greater influence in Ireland than the voice of the Vatican itself. Without the benefit of Foucault's teaching on historical reconstruction, we would not now be able to explain exactly why the CDF was trying to efface this particular discontinuity: we would not see that power/knowledge was again working beneficially to pursue its struggle for truth. Small wonder that the CDF insisted that Flannery should not attend the meetings of the ACP and that he should withdraw for extended periods of reflection and reconsideration.

But, of course, power/knowledge is not always a positive connection. Flannery now finds himself stranded and suspended. His domain has become 'Limbo, 21st century style'. But at least, as I found, he can look at himself in the mirror. The Vatican, in contrast – and particularly in contrast with the compassion of Pope Francis – is looking suspect. And a widening number of observers are attentive to media leaks suggesting that conservative interests in the Church have been too strong for our current Pope to overthrow.

We said earlier that 'domain' is discourse stripped of its discursive trail, the pure description of the facts of the discourse at that point in time; the discursive relations might form part of this domain but the discursive practices did not. And that something in that domain gives rise to the actor's dissent. In contrast with my own experience, Flannery's dissent was actually directed at discursive relations, at the CDF's despicable attempt to suborn his own personal belief as expressed through Vatican II.

The wise manager or administrator, detecting a similar pattern of events should now be able to imagine a wider range of options than if he or she had merely thought in terms of a dissident Galway priest who upset the powers that be.

As explained in the Preface, I was not able to engage with Fr Flannery so as to bring Giddens's deeper insight to bear upon the conclusion stated above. This is a limitation of this investigation but one, I think, that was unavoidable and can be respected.

Chapter 6
Case Study 3 - Peter Oborne

For Peter Oborne, the apparent cause of his dissent was clear and well-publicised. In the instinctive manner of an experienced journalist setting out the essence of his article in a short, pithy headline statement, he declared to followers of *www.opendemocracy.net*:

> The coverage of HSBC in Britain's [*Daily*] *Telegraph* is a fraud on its readers. If major newspapers allow corporations to influence their content for fear of losing advertising revenue, democracy itself is in peril[42].

Here speaks the practised journalist and political commentator on a subject close to his heart – withholding information where there should be complete transparency and, furthermore, manipulating content, all to the ultimate detriment of the political system which allows that essential freedom of the press.

Oborne was speaking at the end of a journey of increasing unease and mounting disquiet. Noticeably, he was also speaking from that same moral standpoint that so exercised Flannery and me. They were all speaking from the centre of their being on something they cared sufficiently passionately about to stand up when other witnesses retreated.

42

https://www.opendemocracy.net/ourkingdom/peteroborne/whyihaveresignedfromt elegraph - Mr Oborne's post-resignation blog statement from which all quotes shown have been taken.

But remember how, with Flannery and me, Foucault enabled us to shift the initially understood cause of our dissent on to something different. This is not to say that Foucault changed what we were saying: it is that Foucault enabled us to change our understanding of what we were saying.

In my case, my motivation seemed to originate in the unpreparedness of local government for a major flood and in the ineptness of the following response. I was even resentful of that incompetence, knowing that I could have done better if I had been managing the response to that crisis. But we were next able to restate the cause of my dissent as persistent gross officialdom, over many years, affecting the same under-privileged group of people – people with whom he had become intimately involved. And, with Giddens's assistance, we could reduce that sustained subjugation to the unawareness of, or perhaps even indifference to, the situation of very poor people trying to make sense of shattered lives while being knee-deep in sewage and human waste and not knowing how to decontaminate and protect themselves.

In Flannery's case, our first understanding was *tout court* a question of conscience. And what greater reason can there be, so today's busy executive might decide, for *not* pursuing a problem any further than that a west of Ireland parish priest cannot sleep at night? With Foucault's help however, Flannery's crisis could actually be seen to rest upon the CDF's deliberate, sustained attempt to suborn Flannery's beliefs, as expressed through the only authentic re-statement of faith for several centuries (Vatican II) – and in doing so, the CDF was using power arrogated to itself, and *not* power 'as a practice' of the Church to which Flannery had pledged his existence. Now, that is a cause for further reflection.

So, what can Foucault tell us about Oborne's case that was not apparent in his published, headline statement, set out above? Let us begin with 'the ground under his feet'.

First, we learn of his immense pride at being invited to undertake the role of Chief Political Commentator "in the most important conservative-leaning newspaper in Britain". The conservative perspective was overwhelmingly important to Oborne. His family had brought him up in that tradition. By way of demonstration and right up there in the opening paragraphs, Oborne specifically refers to his grandfather, quoting his army rank (Lieutenant Colonel) and status as a recipient of the Distinguished Service Order (DSO), and explaining that he used to read the *Daily Telegraph* leading articles at breakfast each morning. Why, we should ask, did he choose to profile that?

The DSO is an immediately recognisable, senior honour for British military officers of any of the three services, awarded for meritorious or distinguished service, typically in actual combat. But only a Briton with certain class and social affiliations would unthinkingly make mention of it – because, within that circle, people like Oborne's grandfather are regularly referred to in that way. In other words, pride in a relative's achievement is still there but it has been augmented by the attendant social practices. Consider also what the related discourse of rank tells us: Oborne's grandfather is a 'half-Colonel' (Oborne didn't use that quintessential phrase from the Officers' Mess but he could well have done). Being a 'half', or Lieutenant, Colonel means that someone has progressed by selection to the first rung of the upper military class and not through promotion on a 'time-served' basis. So, there is a bit of one-upmanship as well as legitimate, familial pride[43].

Then note that this much respected forbear used to read the *Daily Telegraph* at breakfast, apparently over his bacon and eggs. There are several statements embedded here: the newspaper is delivered and not collected in person (this used to be a widespread practice but it still says something about the household); breakfast is, by construction, something of a family affair (you all sit down together implying a settled, semi-formal routine); breakfast is cooked and, furthermore, traditional (implying wealth and permanence); the grandfather, being presumably the head of the family, is allowed to read at the same time that others are eating (which some, today, might think was rather disrespectful to the remainder at the table but, then, was very much accepted); and what he was reading were the 'leaders', in other words the opinion-forming part of the newspaper.[44]

---

[43] Half-Colonels, like Commanders in the Royal Navy and Wing Commanders in the Royal Air Force, have a bit of gold braid around the peaks of their caps. A highly prized status symbol, I can tell you.

[44] I feel the need to emphasise, for the benefit of any incredulous reader, that this whole paragraph is not some music hall caricature (although the late Peter Ustinov did tell an outrageous but revealing story on the subject). The content of this paragraph is central to the way in which people of a certain age and class still happen to think in Britain – and Peter Oborne and younger cohorts, too, I imagine, are evidently part of it. If an Irish reader needs a parallel for the intensity of this way of thinking and behaving, remember the discourse of the Civil War and how some families today are still fiercely Fine Gael and others Fianna Fáil: these affiliations entail ways of thinking about one's situation and one's obligations

The unwritten impression in everything Oborne reveals of himself is of family fortune, unchanging practices, innate conservatism, middle class tradition, received opinion and, therefore, a way of thinking about the world that, as anyone who is anyone knows, only the *Daily Telegraph* can reliably put into words.

Small wonder, then, that this same grandfather had been influential in the local Conservative Association and was archetypical of the sort of people Oborne knew were also followers of the *Daily Telegraph*. He imagines these ideal types when drafting his articles: he wrote with them in mind and even schooled himself before taking up his appointment in the skills and techniques (the 'knowledges') of the great journalists to have held that same responsibility before him:

> I was very conscious that I was joining a formidable tradition of political commentary. I spent my summer holiday before taking up my duties as columnist reading the essays of the great Peter Utley, edited by Charles Moore and Simon Heffer, two other masters of the art. No one has ever expressed quite as well as Utley the quiet decency and pragmatism of British conservatism.

For Irish readers, it is important to explain that such passion and respect for both the middle class political tradition and the national newspaper which was its mouthpiece, is not unusual in the Britain of decades past. To many participants, this remains a discourse of 'what made Britain great', 'what took us through the war'[45] and 'what will keep us great to-

---

which remain very real to the families involved. Why, for example, do some people still go to pay their respects every August at Béal na mBláth?

[45] It might also be argued that what took Britain through the war was a complex, fortuitous mix of widely diverse qualities including the powerful interplay between the middle and working classes, a distinguishable and indomitable sense of humour, the traditions and bloody-mindedness of institutions, the self-belief that comes from living on an island, a passionate belief in British independence and supremacy, and a willing but sometimes grudging respect for royalty. Winston Churchill came into it, too, as did America and the British Commonwealth and the excellence of its sailors, soldiers and airmen. But the point for Oborne is that the discourse of conservative values, epitomised by the *Daily Telegraph*,

day'. Its strength must never be underestimated. It deserves its place in any sociological reckoning.

To this 'ground under the feet' of Peter Oborne needs now to be added the intrinsic quality of the newspaper itself. In addition to "the formidable tradition of political commentary" (above), Oborne adds "integrity … [and] … superb news coverage". The *Daily Telegraph* had even recently smashed wide open a scandal of MPs' expenses, situated in the very class interests that are described in the two preceding pages, and was demonstrably a voice that all could trust:

> The *Mail* is raucous and populist, while the *Times* is proud to swing with the wind as the voice of the official class. The [*Daily*] *Telegraph* stood in a different tradition. It is read by the nation as a whole, not just by the City and Westminster. It is confident of its own values. It has long been famous for the accuracy of its news reporting.

Small wonder that Oborne was immensely proud at being appointed to such a senior role. And yet all was not well with the newspaper. Circulation was falling quickly when he joined it in September 2010 and Oborne believes that the owners had been "panicked" into believing that digital, rather than print, communication was now the way ahead. A wave of sackings followed despite "a very healthy circulation of more than half a million". On more than one occasion, Oborne mentioned his concern to the Chief Executive, that the paper was being needlessly destroyed and that the (very loyal) readership should not be taken for granted. But the response was blunt and, on one occasion, offensive: "You don't know what you are fucking talking about."

Whether this was actually gratuitous or a bursting out of intolerable pressure upon the Chief Executive (perhaps in the way that Fr Flannery's Redemptorist Superior was enduring it) was an open question, particularly as the *Daily Telegraph*'s editor, so Oborne explains, had been highly respected and "an excellent editor". But it soon became clear, circumstantially at least, that Oborne's beloved newspaper was indeed being shaken

---

completely infused his family's rich experience of that period and its complex mix, as well as his own personal understanding.

apart in a way that none could have imagined a few years earlier. In the 81 years since between 1923 and 2004, there had been just six editors, all of them outstanding, "towering figures" of journalism. But since the current owners had purchased the newspapers (in 2004), there had been six more. The title 'editor' had been replaced by 'head of content' who worked on weekdays only – which is a staggeringly light, hebdomadal workload for a daily newspaper with a Sunday edition. Next, there were three further 'heads of content' in 2014 alone:

> [Furthermore] for the last 12 months matters have got much, much worse. The foreign desk — magnificent under the leadership of [names] — has been decimated. As all reporters are aware, no newspaper can operate without skilled subeditors. Half of these have been sacked, and the chief sub … has left.

There followed a sequence of absurd errors: "Solecisms, unthinkable until very recently, are now commonplace." And the readers have noticed that these frequently cut across cherished practices and interests in a way that had been hitherto utterly, totally unthinkable:

> … the [Daily] Telegraph took great care to get these things right until very recently. The arrival of [the new head of content] coincided with the arrival of the 'click culture'. Stories seemed no longer judged by their importance, accuracy or appeal to those who actually bought the paper. The more important measure appeared to be the number of online visits. On 22 September, the [Daily] Telegraph online ran a story about a woman with three breasts. One despairing executive told me that it was known this was false even before the story was published. I have no doubt it was published in order to generate online traffic, at which it may have succeeded. I am not saying that online traffic is unimportant, but over the long term, however, such episodes inflict incalculable damage on the reputation of the paper.

Oborne's disbelief was mounting. Next he found that the distinction between advertising and editorial, a rigorously enforced division of activity that was fundamental to impartial journalism, had not just collapsed but had apparently been pulled down. A number of his reports were 'spiked', particularly where commercial giants were the object of his scrutiny. Oborne checked further: had he said something that was legally awkward? But no, there was never a problem of that sort – only the strengthening impression, through reading between the lines, that certain client interests were systematically protected by the owners' representatives from critical comment by the editorial staff.

Oborne's extended entry on the Open Democracy website gives the detail of this gathering storm and outrage. But then came an even more serious affront to everything the newspaper stood for and everything that Oborne considered the readership expected:

> At the start of December the *Financial Times*, the *Times* and the *Guardian* all wrote powerful leaders on the refusal by the Chinese government to allow a committee of British MPs into Hong Kong. The [*Daily*] *Telegraph* remained silent. I can think of few subjects which anger and concern [*Daily*] *Telegraph* readers more.

Significantly, the *Telegraph* then published a commentary by the Chinese ambassador, juxtaposed with the lucrative *China Watch* supplement to the newspaper[46]. The headline of the ambassador's article was: 'Let's not allow Hong Kong to come between us'. In other words, the *Daily Telegraph* newspaper was now demonstrably allowing Chinese interests to leverage the promise of increased commercial activity over the truth – and it had always been the truth on which the integrity of the newspaper had habitually hung.

Other instances followed and Oborne soon offered his resignation. Note that this was not dissent – for example, he was invited to write a weekly column[47] by way of working out his notice. But his sense of ontological insecurity, first expressed as concern that the new owners were

---

[46] Lucrative through advertising revenue – Chinese advertising revenue.

[47] Remember what Hannah Arendt advised: if you are not dissenting, you are consenting. And what more persuasive sign of consent can there be than continuing to write for the newspaper?

destroying this unique, cherished and conservative newspaper, had now reached the point where he had no alternative but to resign "as a matter of conscience".

This was close to dissent (as well as being close to Flannery's question of conscience) but not yet close enough.

Separately, Oborne continued to investigate whether advertising interests had ever been allowed to influence editorial content before – and then, suddenly, his weekly column was cut off altogether, although his notice period would still be respected. Not wishing to cause difficulties for his recent colleagues, Oborne accepted the situation and began preparing himself mentally "for the alluring prospect of several months paid gardening leave."

But then, the BBC *Panorama* programme ran a story about HSBC and its Swiss banking arm, alleging a wide-scale tax evasion scheme. 'HSBC files' were being published left, right and centre and, soon, all the London newspapers realised that this was a major event:

> The *FT* splashed on it for two days in a row, while the *Times* and the *Mail* gave it solid coverage spread over several pages. [But] you needed a microscope to find the [*Daily*] *Telegraph* coverage: nothing on Monday, six slim paragraphs at the bottom left of page two on Tuesday, seven paragraphs deep in the business pages on Wednesday. The [*Daily*] *Telegraph's* reporting only looked up when the story turned into claims that there might be questions about the tax affairs of people connected to the Labour party.

Oborne had earlier experienced one of his investigations into HSBC being 'spiked' by the *Daily Telegraph* – and the latest development served to take him finally to the point of dissent:

> [Most reluctantly] I have come to the conclusion that I have a duty to make all this public. There are two powerful reasons. The first concerns the future of the [*Daily*] *Telegraph* under [its current owners]. It might sound a pompous thing to say, but I believe the newspaper is a significant part of Britain's civic architecture. It is the most important public

voice of civilised, sceptical conservatism. [*Daily*] *Telegraph* readers are intelligent, sensible, well-informed people. They buy the newspaper because they feel that they can trust it. If advertising priorities are allowed to determine editorial judgments, how can readers continue to feel this trust? The [*Daily*] *Telegraph's* recent coverage of HSBC amounts to a form of fraud on its readers. It has been placing what it perceives to be the interests of a major international bank above its duty to bring the news to [*Daily*] *Telegraph* readers. There is only one word to describe this situation: terrible. ...

... a second and even more important point ... bears not just on the fate of one newspaper but on public life as a whole. A free press is essential to a healthy democracy. There is a purpose to journalism, and it is not just to entertain. It is not to pander to political power, big corporations and rich men. Newspapers have what amounts in the end to a constitutional duty to tell their readers the truth.

Meanwhile Oborne continued digging. He soon found that, for some two years, adverse stories about the HSBC bank had been routinely abandoned as soon as its lawyers became involved. Journalists were then ordered to destroy records and files. Next, lawyers for the *Daily Telegraph's* owners became involved – and from that point onwards, *any* story critical of the HSBC was discouraged if not disabled. Even reports of criminal acts were allegedly suppressed.

Oborne is helpfully complete in his explanations and we do not need to devil much at what he is telling us. His dissent followed the truth that "any editorial operation that is clearly influenced by advertising is classic appeasement. Once a very powerful body knows they can exert influence they know they can come back and threaten you." But we still have not achieved clarity on the actual reason for dissent – and only Foucault can illuminate that.

Consider, therefore, the question of knowledges subjugated by the discourse of commercial profitability – unhelpful interruptions to that continuous, purged reconstitution of events. These knowledges came from Oborne and like-minded colleagues. They came in the tradition of the great journalists who preceded them. But was not Oborne also carrying deep in his psyche an *inherited* knowledge? Remember the man who read the newspaper while eating his breakfast every day – a man who had, somewhere in his locker, a medal for conspicuous bravery, a man whom a loving grandson revered. Perhaps they used the salt cellar and pepper pot together, in between the bacon and eggs, to re-imagine particular wartime battles? Remember also the small people, the farmers, the shop-keepers, the people whom Oborne thought of every day as he wrote his editorials – people who had fought alongside his grandfather and fought through eventually to victory. These were people who trusted that they would always be told the truth, people who had demonstrated that they would never be subjugated.

In that same vein, Oborne's predecessors, the ghosts in the offices of the old *Daily Telegraph*, had always fought and fought well for the audience at the centre of Oborne's consciousness. But now it was his turn. It was his lot to witness the sudden, unwelcome subjugation of their erudite knowledge by the newly intrusive discursive relations of a discourse of power and continuing profitability. And Oborne had no alternative but to stand up and fight in turn.

Foucault tells us that Oborne was fighting his own battle *against* the lawyers as externalities and against the detested priorities of the owners they represented – and *for* the tradition he had been brought up in. He was fighting, as his grandfather had fought, so that tyranny would not prevail. He was standing up in that same, proud and fiercely resilient tradition. He was standing up because he could not let that same tradition down. By fighting, he was taking back, to its rightful owners, the power within that the new intruders were steadily usurping and destroying for the benefit of their bottom line.

Oborne, like me, also needed to be able to look in 'the mirror'. It is just that Oborne's mirror was assembled during tales of valour, empire and struggle for survival, and was passed down to a small boy over breakfast paraphernalia at the family dining table – while mine lay somewhere in the waters of the River Shannon and the traditions of small people who went that way to fish and to share their harvest with even poorer people still. Flannery's mirror lay somewhere in that mystical abandonment of every worldly desire in favour of a life of denial and priestly service – service to the supreme teaching of Vatican II.

Once again, it is Foucault who enables us to go this far. It is Foucault who enables us to reach the point beyond which no further refinement is necessary. What did he tell us in that extraordinary, impenetrable sentence included in the Introduction? *A point where "knowledge grounds its positivity and thereby manifests a history ...*" Like a flash of lightning, the stored-up energy is suddenly discharged and we see, illuminated before us, the hidden history we have been searching for and its embedded memory of triumph over adversity and its readiness for more. "*Such an enterprise,*" continues Foucault, "*is not so much a history, in the traditional meaning of that word, as an 'archaeology'*" (2002: xxiv).

How similar in many respects to Flannery's situation and, to some extent, to mine. Is it not a reasonable conclusion that this third Case Study is actually confirming what the first two told us in their separate ways? Unfortunately, and as explained at the end of Case Study 2 in Fr Flannery's case, I was not able to engage with Peter Oborne so as to bring Giddens's deeper insight to bear upon the conclusion stated above. I did not actually feel, in any case, that I needed to. I believed that Foucault had taken me as far as I needed to go and that Oborne would be disinclined to delve any deeper.

Chapter 7

Case Study 4 - Ignazio Silone

Silone (1900-1978) was borne in the Italian Abruzzo and, after earlier losing his father, finally orphaned during an earthquake at the age of 15 years. He was a teenage militant active in the Young Socialists during the First World War and became a founder member of the Italian Communist Party after the Young Socialists split in 1921. A contemporary of Gramsci, Silone's demonstrably Christian basis can, self-evidently, be distinguished from the former's theoretical Marxism (see Pugliesi, 2009: 74 *et seq.* for a discussion of their differences and Gramsci's "fundamental ambiguity").

As a bright young personality, Silone began to make regular contact with the Communist movement in Berlin and Moscow and soon came into contact with Lenin and Trotsky. He was sent back to Italy to combat the growth of Fascism but was eventually expelled from the Italian Communist party for unhelpful sympathies. A natural follower of Trotsky, it is convenient to assume that he, too, fell foul of Stalin's growth in power and became an eventual casualty of Trotsky's condemnation in 1927. By 1923, however, he found himself in a Spanish prison where he was incarcerated for helping the local community. At this point he felt able to discard his birth name (Secondino Tranquilli) and reimagine himself as Ignazio Silone[48]. As Silone, he began to reorient himself towards a path of moral criticism and realist writing (Foot, 2000).

Having rejoined the Socialist Party in Switzerland in 1941, he was next imprisoned by the Swiss authorities on spurious, manufactured rumours circulated from Moscow. This is the period in which he wrote the work *Notes from a Swiss Prison* on which, drawn from *Bitter Spring*, the dissent investigation in this Chapter is largely based. This investigation is mostly

---

[48] The Christian name, Secondino, meant 'prison guard' in the Abruzzo dialect which, we can speculate, must have been anathema to him.

referred to in subsequent paragraphs as 'Pugliesi' who translated Silone and authored *Bitter Spring*, and has a substantial reputation as an historian. The point being made is that, unlike case studies 1 to 3, Pugliesi and Silone are together conducting the investigation of dissent, not the author of this book.

By 1944, Silone was back in Rome and taking an active part in Socialist Party politics. By the end of that decade, however, he had split with both the Socialists and with any Communist link and was firmly associated with emerging Cold War positions. He seems, for example, to have come into the circle of Allen Dulles of the Office of Strategic Services (later the CIA) and, then, the Head of US Station in Berne, and of Eleanor Roosevelt, the wife of the American President.

Silone enjoyed a considerable reputation as a novelist, particularly in the 1930s and 40s, but actually became more interesting for our purposes some ten years after his death: evidence that he had been a police informer between 1928 and 1930, if not earlier, was produced. Two Italian historians, Biocca and Canali, unearthed written proof which caused huge controversy at the time and then grudging acceptance that Silone must have had some contact with the police during those difficult years. The evidence took the form of two letters from which Foot quotes as follows:

> ... the writer speaks of a deep moral and psychological crisis, and pleads to be released from 'all falsehood, doubt and secrecy', expressing a desire 'to repair the damage that I have caused, to seek redemption, to help the workers, the peasant (to whom I am bound with every fibre in my body) and my country.
> (*ibid.*)

More bombshells were to follow. The indisputable truth was that Silone was indeed a secret police informer from 1919 to 1930 – and that Italy was completely rocked by the revelations 50 years and more later. But the immensely useful thing is that the two researchers investigating Silone felt able to trace his moral and psychological crises to the incarceration in 1928 and later death of his younger brother in prison in 1932. Their account and assessment are definitive. Much may remain to be discovered about Silone's career between the war years but we can feel reasonably safe in assuming that the tide had turned in the years before 'Pugliesi' and that all Silone was producing by the time of his own incarceration in Switzerland was the truth, if only a therapeutic form:

> I passed from fear of punishment to fear of non-punishment. The idea that I was haunted by the wrong I had done only because of the continual risk of being found out began to frighten me. So, I began to wonder whether, if better technique enabled one to betray one's friends with the certainty that one would never be found out, that would make it more supportable ... So, might technique be capable of destroying the distinction between right and wrong, by eliminating the risk of punishment? The idea frightens me. (Drake, 2009, citing Leake)

Foot reports that from the ensuing psychological breakdown came the "distinguished writer and pillar of anti-fascism the world has thought it knew ever since." That may be as close to the real self as any investigation into the reasons for dissent may ever aspire to come. Most helpfully, it allows Giddens to say: "Start digging in that decade – don't dig any earlier." This is supported by Drake's analysis of Leake's assessment of Silone's novel *Bread and Wine* (*ibid.*). Silone's emergence as something fundamentally more honest and even "existential" was by then complete.

Richard Drake tells us that in the years after the Second World War until his death, Silone was admired by George Orwell, whom we have already suggested was a mid-20th century dissenter. Orwell shared many of Silone's ideological, essentially pro-socialist viewpoints and thought of him as "an independent-minded man naturally inclined to go against the grain of every orthodoxy" (2009). This is consistent with the existential, critical impression of dissent that we have begun to form. To be sure, Orwell's opinion was before the bombshells of the 1990s but in him we have one more endorsement of Silone as reliable material for analysis at this point in his life.

The strengths of Pugliesi, for Drake, include "a sensitive awareness of the ways in which Christianity survived in Silone's mature thinking" (which we might categorise as principle or moral truth); greater depth, relatively speaking in the later stages of Silone's life; and some highly important contributions to our understanding of the writer's personal life From Silone's wife, there is some "vivid testimony about the punishing effects on their marriage of Silone's depression, melancholy, cruelty, and

infidelities". Being incapable of meaningful relationships, the consequence was that Silone enriched his writing by cramming everything he
had to say about humanity into his writing (*ibid.*). This is highly significant. As indicated above, it means that, in this Chapter, Silone and
Pugliesi were only ever going to lead us through some very rich material
while Foucault and Giddens watched approvingly.

Most importantly, Pugliesi writes as a fair-minded defender of Silone
who does not avoid the evidence: "...he offers intelligent and balanced
observations about the major spokesmen from the prosecution and the
defence in the Silone case." Furthermore, "the truth in the Silone case, or
as close to the truth as we can get" is that Silone's work remains a "powerful testament to a struggle for justice and liberty".

It is worth noting, too, that Pugliesi also draws parallels between Silone
and, variously, Mahatma Gandhi, Martin Luther King, George Orwell
(*ibid.*: 8 and 11) and even Jean-Paul Sartre (*ibid.*: 15). His politics reflected
"humanistic socialism combined with compassionate libertarianism"
(*ibid.*: 7). So, Silone was emphatically located in the grain already described in Chapter 2 of this book. But it is the three concepts in the preceding paragraphs, above – humanity, justice and liberty – that have been
used to approach *Bitter Spring* and Pugliesi's analyses to confirm their
consistency with Giddens's method, for further insights into dissent and
for deeper clues to the ground under the feet of Silone. It might then have
remained for either Foucault or Giddens, or both, to sift further if Silo-
ne/Pugliesi had not done so first.

Pugliesi tells us that, at the moment when Silone was 'born', the imprisoned Secondino, was reading Dostoevsky. We cannot readily discount,
therefore, a lasting influence of the latter upon the young Tranquilli's reimagined personality[49]: "Life is in ourselves and not in the external," wrote
Dostoevsky to his brother (1849) following a moment of great crisis – a
crisis that was difficult, challenging and supremely arduous for the poor.
That was Tranquilli's experience, too. It is unlikely to be coincidence,
then, that the man Silone reinvented in that Spanish prison cell was an
avenger, "a curious mixture of priest and communist" charged with "the
absolute necessity of bearing witness" (Pugliesi, 2009: 3).

---

[49] See, for example, Pugliesi, 2009: 19 and 78 *et seq.*.

Silone's was a profoundly moral vision of the world but the 'trajectory' of that vision, for Pugliesi, lay towards "some ambiguously[50] mapped terrain between memoir, literature and history" (*ibid.*: 13).

Pugliesi tells us repeatedly that the 'terrain' was and remained Pescina, the site of Silone's upbringing and of the terrible earthquake that took the lives of his mother and all but one of his remaining siblings (see, for example, *ibid.*: 82). The 'memoir', we are told (*ibid.*: 47) was threefold: first, the earthquake and what it did to his remaining family, together with the role played by the Priest Don Orione (now St Luigi Orione) in gathering the children affected; second, the arrest, imprisonment, torture and death of his younger brother (in which Don Orione again was active in the background for the efforts he made to steer the young Romolo Tranquilli away from trouble); and, third, Silone's expulsion from the Italian Communist Party in 1931. The 'literature' may be glimpsed in repeated, unhelpful accounts of the Abruzzo and Pescina (which Silone overturned himself when paying tribute to the enormous potential, courage and generosity of the local population). The young Tranquilli had been himself frequently reminded that, as a peasant, he was of the *cafoni*[51]– "flesh used to suffering" (*ibid.*: 36), crushed, sorrowful, worthless etc. etc. And the 'history' lay in the massive corruption that characterised the dispersal of earthquake and other relief funds, particularly through the Church. Indeed, the Church as Silone recalled it bore little comparison to the peasant stories and Christmas rituals practised in the much, and unjustly, abused Pescina. It taught the young to submit and endure, to mind their own business and keep their profile low. The State was even worse: in the eyes of the Italian peasant, it stood for "theft, corruption and special privilege" (*ibid.*: 58).

Only Don Orione seemed different and his constant presence in the background enables us to re-imagine 'terrain' as the whole context for Silone's work and motivation. Silone once, unhesitatingly, compared Orione to Lenin when asked if he had ever come across anyone else with such

---

[50] It is the view of this book that Silone's terrain became quite clear and unambiguous, as the following paragraph suggests and as the express comparisons with later western European personalities, in preceding chapters would seem to confirm, too. Pugliesi's reference to "ambiguous" is taken to refer to the earlier years, before he was 'outed' as a secret police informer.

[51] *Cafone* (plural *cafoni*) is a pejorative Italian expression for someone who is ignorant and primitive.

a temperament and personality and replied: "Lenin. I have met no-one else of the intellectual stature of those two men, combined with the same magnetic and rebellious personality and the same immense drive. Don Orione might easily have been a Lenin" (*ibid.*: 52). Lenin may have been a controversial figure but, helpfully, his huge personality was also opposed to the totalitarian power of Stalin and he did champion workers' rights and freedoms. The value of this personal endorsement, taken with Silone's own sad visits back to Pescina in later life, serve to fix the 'terrain' on which we have to work in truth, justice and liberty – specifically, in truth, justice and liberty for the poor.

In the 1930s, in ill-health and withdrawn to Davos in Switzerland, Silone transitioned from preparing for his life's great œuvre into actually delivering it. He started to write "obeying at all times a strong internal impulse, an authentic necessity" (*ibid.*: 112). He began with the novel *Fontamara*, "... to converse and to remember; to resuscitate in me memories of my people and to share a common sorrow ...". It was to prove "... the most extraordinary, powerful and influential work of anti-Fascist literature of the 1930s" (*ibid.*) in which he used the complete template of the Pescina terrain as the medium for his attack.

Fontamara was a magnificent work of dissent from the shadow falling over Europe – from the rise to power of Hitler and Mussolini. And yet both Foucault and Giddens can take us deeper, and without Silone even mentioning that word 'fascism', than that essentially pan-European decline into the evil that Stefan Zweig was later so memorably to describe (1964). Of course, Pugliesi has done the work for us, using Silone's own accounts and letters – and this is an exception to the rule that is emerging in this short book, that you have to pick up some tools yourself. But it is still the techniques of genealogy and insurrection (Foucault) that can take us sufficiently within Silone's reasons for dissent had the author and his subject not already divulged his specifically Abruzzo focus. Those implements, if unused on this occasion, are still available to us and just as relevant. The choice, whether to take up structuration (Giddens), as well as Foucault's tools, depends entirely upon the degree of fine detail of the duality of rules and resources sought by the craftsman or woman – as, for example, in the final dénouement in *Fontamara* over what to call a *cafone* newspaper. *What is to be done* they decided and, with that same statement hanging over every other issue facing them, says Silone, came the moment of liberation. That is, structure and agency in perfect, enabling harmony.

But don't turn away yet. Doesn't the consistency of Foucault and Giddens with Pugliesi's analyses firmly remind us again that it was indeed Pescina Silone was concerned for all the time? So when did Nazi Germany and Fascist Italy begin to edge out Pescina from the tale? When did the discourse of socialist, anti-totalitarianism literature in the mid-20th century arrogate *Fontamara* to itself? The truth is that it doesn't matter in the slightest. Silone's work was only ever authentic dissent about Pescina, about "swindling land-owners and corrupt administrators" (Pugliesi, 2009: 120, citing Graham Greene). Nazi Germany and Fascist Italy were simply a coincidence in time – other examples of contemporary, totalitarian violence and atrocities, if profoundly worse ones in scale.

Chronologically speaking, the next great successes for Silone were *Bread and Wine*, written in the mid-1930s, then *The Seed Beneath the Snow* and next *The Third Front* during the early years of World War II. The latter was a call to arms to the Italian population to rise up and overthrow the rampant corruption and oppression of two failed decades of totalitarianism under Mussolini, who promised a corporate State but in fact so dreadfully ruined Italy, dragging its people into the shadow of the Swastika and all that that stood for.

But look, it is the ground under his feet again that Silone is addressing, not the prevailing international implications of the Allied war effort within which his work is conveniently assimilated: "It was time for the Italian people to reclaim *their* human dignity, *their* honour as free citizens rather than degraded subjects, and to reassert *their* own natural rights" (*ibid.*: 143, italics added). And he meant it: he wasn't talking about European battlefield plans or military stratagems or Allied politics, but of his experiences in the Abruzzo that still remained so vivid. Silone urged civil disobedience in order that the *Italian* people should reclaim liberty by themselves. Each citizen would find his own way. By connecting the political challenges of their country to a moral task for each citizen, a widening campaign of civil disobedience would "transform anti-fascism" (*ibid.*: 144).

Simultaneously with this call to demonstrate a wide dissent, however, Silone was 'set up' extraordinarily by Stalin who found Silone's Christian prescriptions inconvenient to the preferred Moscow line. This dark initiative could only oblige the Swiss authorities to arrest Silone who was now identified unjustifiably as a traitor to the regime that had succoured him for more than a decade. He *was*, demonstrably, a defender of liberty and democracy but, in the midst of war-torn Europe, he now found himself labelled subversive and thrown to the wolves for whatever hidden purposes that part of the Soviet machine thought appropriate (*ibid*.: 146).

And it is here that we stand back and allow Silone to lead us further on his own investigation, so redolent of the Foucault-Giddens approach, of his own solitary voice (*ibid*.: 150 *et seq*.).

Writing in prison, he reviews his loyalty to the Swiss State and authorities[52] and strips bare the lies and promises of the Italian fascist regime, the demise of which was even in 1942 becoming obvious. But then he turns to the future and his dissent turns against the ground being laid through the assumptions for post-war politics and agreement. It was not the machinery of post-war settlement, he declared, but the Italian working classes who would decide their future. In effect, he breaks his promise to the Swiss Police not to engage in politics, with the effect that the solitary voice, an authentic voice freed at last from its turmoil, was then heard speaking clearly.

In addition to its clarity, Silone's was a remarkable, passionate *tour d'horizon* before a Swiss nation which had enjoyed democracy for 750 years, and also an urgent demand that its people recognise his "essentially ethical" stance. He stood for the complete rejection of solutions based on conventional prescriptions, and for a spiritual hunger for truth and moral reform (*ibid*.: 152). His speaking out was a matter of conscience, standing up against the bolshevist attempt to suborn the path of grass-roots, Italian Socialism and saying "No!" Imploring the Swiss police not to prejudice the safety of Italian free-thinkers and anti-fascists whose names and addresses were to be found among his (confiscated) papers, Silone finally declares: "I have spoken and freed my spirit ... I hope not to be read by a policeman but by a man and a Christian" (*ibid*.: 153).

In Chapter 3 of *Bitter Spring*, Silone himself, superbly assisted by Pugliesi, has taken us down the path of archaeological investigation and even exposed for our edification the processes by which social life in the Pescina was recursively implicated and, in Silone's heart, preserved as a tragedy to be avenged. But, for the purposes of this book, Foucault and Giddens would never have allowed us to stray from that same path if Silone and Pugliesi had, perchance, allowed an invalid, distracting set of signposts to stand. We can see a short but effective demonstration of this as-

---

[52] We considered these in Chapter 2, above.

sertion in Silone's experience on his return to Italy in 1944 when he found that the stories he had created were no longer his own – the characters had evolved. Accordingly, he commenced a major re-editing task to get back to the truth, a process he likened to "Michelangelo's conception of sculpture: *remove excess marble to reveal the trapped human figure within*" (*ibid.:* 161, italics added). Foucault might have said: *dig down to free those subjugated knowledges.* And Giddens: *re-establish where the duality of the rules and resources that allowed this person to transform his or her situation was still intact.*

Indeed, they were all talking about the same thing.

Chapter 8

Discussion

This Chapter begins with some brief reflections upon the four case studies. First, there was the opening suggestion in Chapter 1 that Foucault and Giddens together would have a considerable impact upon the analyses in Case Study1; that Foucault only would prove usable on the material available in Case Studies 2 and 3; but that Foucault and Giddens would have worked well together again in Case Study 4, had not Silone/Pugliesi led the way. That superficial introduction can now be improved upon.

Second, then, it becomes possible to attribute a more thoughtful reason for generally distinguishing Case Studies 1 and 4 on the one hand, from Case Studies 2 and 3 on the other. Recalling the other early advice from Chapter 1, that with a little practice it is possible to follow Foucault's methods unnoticed, like a yoga exercise, it becomes possible to suggest that numbers 2 and 3 are where the corporate reader should focus most of his or her attention. The reader seeking greater insight – and having more time to delve more deeply – should turn to numbers 1 and 4. That could be one reason and, as far as it goes, it seems valid: Case Studies 2 and 3 demonstrate how to dig quickly and confidently to the point where a usable explanation for the solitary dissent under investigation has been liberated. But another reason must lie in the plain evidence that Silone/Pugliesi were actually doing what Foucault/Giddens would have done had there been no intermediary to demonstrate (as in Case Study 1) the link between ontological insecurity and the eventual dissent.

We do not need, therefore, to start to sift the exposed sediment in Case Studies 1 and 4 all over again because the job has been done already and done well. It were better to reflect on the method than on turning over, needlessly, ground already sifted.

This Chapter continues, therefore, by drawing some preliminary statements from Case Studies 2 and 3 which, taken together, tend to reinforce the seriousness the Irish Attorney General attached to the "principled, dissenting voice". These statements are based upon the reasonable premise that the fact of solitary dissent means that something really has gone wrong within the context, rather than within the person now complaining. The list is written with the corporate professional in mind and may be all that he or she requires. Next, the Chapter offers a cross-check with Flyvbjerg's account of his dissent from planning practices in Danish Aalborg in order to establish whether this is ground that has been covered before – and observes *en passant* that Flyvbjerg is offering substantial endorsement indeed for the interpretation of Foucault that has been distilled and put to work here. The Chapter makes the most of that opportunity by summarising the Foucault approach at a higher level of scholarship than has thus far been attempted: it is, if you like, the author's way of setting Foucault alongside Giddens so that the latter's finishing-up method can be seen in complete context, can be compared with Foucault and can be shown to be startlingly different. This is doubly important to accomplish. The exercise explains, by reference to established theorists, what Silone/Pugliesis were doing in respect of the Abruzzo and Pescina; and it demonstrates that the subject's use of Giddens's method in Case Study 1 is consistent with that in Case Study 4.

Let us return then to our initial set of propositions:

1. The solitary voice dissenting is likely to follow the experience of mounting concern, which may have lasted weeks, months or possibly longer. In principle, therefore, there is a 'window' within which something could have, and possibly still can, be done to resolve the reason for dissent. In other words, wise management and administration may care to invest, cautiously, in mechanisms that enable incipient dissent to be aired.

2. If there is likely to be a negative impact from an insurrection of knowledges expressed through dissent, then any intervention, which identifies that concern is mounting and dissent is possible but first finds a way of accommodating it, may be presumed to have a positive outcome.

3. Factors affecting the individual's conversion of mounting concern into dissent may be social or professional, or both. But there is room, too, for some more deeply ingrained instinct that this book calls, for convenience but without scientific precision, 'genetic'. Taken together, these factors may be quite richly nuanced and a story in themselves. At their core, however, will lie a strong, moral conviction.

4. Identifying mounting concern and what to do about it would seem to be more reliably accomplished by working *from* discourse and genealogy, which can be analysed (relatively) objectively, *to* individual factors

such as the social, professional and 'genetic', which are subjective and may even be withheld.

5. Notwithstanding its duration, the final conversion of mounting concern into dissent may occur quite quickly – for example, when the hypothetical witness is suddenly motivated to stand up. The 'window' may close if action is postponed much further. It is not the speed of conversion that matters however. It is the fact that mounting concern has now been converted into dissent which is important. Unattended, concern may possibly go away but dissent will not.

6. It is likely that the person now dissenting will have a relationship with the author(s) of events that led to the dissent – and that greater power over the relationship will lie with the author(s) of those events, not with the person now dissenting.

7. The question of responsibility for the dissent that has arisen first attaches, therefore, to the person with greater power over that pre-existing relationship. It follows that staff training might reasonably give some priority to developing management's sensitivity to mounting concern and to appropriate response mechanisms.

8. Although the dissenter must take responsibility for his or her decision (to stand up and express dissent), the origin of the dissent may be traceable to the actions of another. The origin may even be scattered across a number of collaborating agencies. Where responsibility lies for corrective action may not always be clear and may even be hidden from the person now dissenting. (By extension, it may even be hidden from the conscientious manager or administrator, too.) It may be argued, therefore, that a second priority for staff training may lie in the development of post-dissent protocols.

9. If the origin of dissent can "be scattered across a number of agencies", Foucault's explication of discourse may well expose a pattern of practices and relations which cut across some precious, individual memory of the person now dissenting – in effect, subjugating his or her personal knowledge.

10. Foucault's explication of genealogy can help illuminate the historical struggle leading to subjugation – and illumination is a good thing. Simultaneously, however, genealogy requires the manager or administrator to step outside the discourse of his or her comfort zone and to open his or her mind to different 'truths'.

11. 'Different truths' are not without institutional problems. It is unlikely to be in the nature of those controlling the manger's or administrator's comfort zone to accept, recognise or even be aware of Foucault's interpretation of discourse and his theorising of genealogy. Structural certainty and the need for continuity will institutionally suppress any possibility of a struggle between competing knowledges and of the risk of discontinuity.

12. 'Moral convictions' are not without difficulty either. A decision needs to be reached by the administrator or manager presented with an instance of solitary dissent (or sensing its imminence) whether the area he or she now needs to enter is an area which, as a matter of corporate policy, should not be pursued any further. In that event, he or she will have to consider extremely carefully any report and recommendations prepared for superiors. Standard complaints procedures may be wholly unsuitable for dealing with the situation: an ethical route out of the problem may need to be devised in order that a future may be contemplated without threat to the mutual respect of all involved. If damaged, this could rebound disadvantageously and unpredictably.

13. But not to heed the solitary voice of dissent must have some impact upon the prevailing structure of power and ultimately on its ends. In effect, dissent will somehow, somewhere, sometime, degrade 'subject susceptibility' unless dissent is accommodated. In other words, the courageous manager or administrator is going to have to take that step away from the hierarchy of accepted knowledge if he wants the present power structure to be preserved and improved.

14. Conversely, the individual memory that has been 'subjugated' need not be limited to the person expressing dissent but may conceivably be a core principle of the organisation itself, which the person now dissenting feels obliged to uphold because it has come under unauthorised pressure. This could suggest that a wider failure of management may have occurred – for example, to communicate new directions – or even that some form of subversive action may now be underway, which the person now dissenting has determined to expose. Discursive relations, to use Foucault's terminology, might be one form of 'subversive action but there may genuinely be an 'attack' from without upon the corporate structure.

15. The effectiveness and sensitivity of governance (and thereby the security of the corporate structure as a whole) could be enhanced by train-

ing in discourse and genealogy, and by exposure to best practice in accommodating or managing dissent. Exceptional alternatives to existing solutions, with an overtly ethical foundation, may need to be devised.

16. It is not clear what best practice in managing solitary dissent might comprise. It is possible that ideas about handling discontinuity may have been 'swallowed up' and 'smoothed over' by the prevailing assumptions of industrial relations, public administration, human resource management or some other official discourse.

17. If these possibilities are accurate, then training in the disciplines mentioned may be deficient, or otherwise skewed towards unquestioning support for discursive practices – and further distorted, or even manipulated unjustifiably, by discursive relations. If these possibilities are not accurate, then everything that has ever been said about that "crucial combination of knowledge and language" (already cited above, and not exclusive to Foucault) could not have been worth the paper it was written on. But such a gross and repeated error of scholarship seems unlikely – and the unconvinced corporate professional is invited to reconsider this section in its entirety before proceeding further.

There is a prestigious precedent for making statements in this way and in this type of situation, where power dominates and normalises in the ways that Foucault understands. The precedent lies in Flyvbjerg's essential 'Aalborg study' on *Rationality and Power: democracy in practice* (1998). Professor Bent Flyvbjerg is an international authority on planning and economic geography, and highly respected for his work in social and political organisation. He is now a world authority at Oxford University. He expressly acknowledges the influence of Foucault and is a champion of his thinking.

Flyvbjerg explained the problem that confronted him in Aalborg as a re-structuring and redevelopment programme to improve the business area of the town, which democratic participation would underpin. And yet the project:

... was transformed by power and [its rationalizations] into environmental degradation and social distortion. Institutions that were supposed to represent what they themselves called "the public interest" were revealed to be deeply em-

bedded in the hidden exercise of power and the protection
of special interests.
(*ibid.*: 225)

While principally a critical examination of democracy in practice, the
Aalborg study also conveys an implicit statement of Flyvbjerg's dissent. By
way of confirmation, Flyvbjerg entitled his consequent compilation of
propositions: "Power has a rationality that rationality does not know"
(*ibid.*: 227 *et seq.*). This is broadly consistent with Case Study 1's analysis of
the time of the Limerick flood. The subject did not recognise, from his
privileged position of close dialogue with the flood-affected residents and
of close observation of events within an environment he had some expert
knowledge of, the validity of what was being said and done: it was 'irra-
tional'. It is broadly consistent, too, with Flannery's observation in Case
Study 2, that the Church was being taken in a direction fundamentally
different from Vatican II – and with Oborne's horror in Case Study 3, that
the content of the *Daily Telegraph* was being steadily manipulated away
from core values and readership interests, and towards dishonest reports
designed to raise the number of 'hits'. For Silone in Case Study 4, it was
the lie and whole distorted history of the alleged worthlessness of the allegedly despicable *cafoni* of Pescina.

It is reasonable, therefore, to compare Flyvbjerg's propositions with
those put forward in the preceding section above, in order to validate the
extent to which weight has already been given to this book's explication of
the way that a greater power can be used. This will confirm for the corporate reader the explanations reached in Case Studies 2 and 3 and in the
discussion given above. Summarised, the complete list of Flyvbjerg's
propositions is:

1. Power defines reality

2. Rationality is context-dependent, the context of rationality
   is power, and power blurs the dividing line between rationality and rationalization

3. Rationalization presented as rationality is a principal strategy in the exercise of power

4. The greater the power, the less the rationality

5. Stable power relations are more typical of politics, administration and planning than antagonistic confrontations

6. Power relations are constantly being produced and reproduced

7. The rationality of power has deeper historical roots than the power of rationality

8. In open confrontation, rationality yields to power

9. Rationality-Power relations are more characteristic of stable power relations than of confrontations

10. The power of rationality is embedded in stable power relations rather than in confrontations

(*ibid.*: 227-234)

Now look back briefly at items 3 and 4 in Flyvbjerg's coherent progression of statements about democracy in practice, above. Items 3 and 4 also encapsulate the difficulties facing the individual driven to declare dissent, specifically:

> ... 'upfront', rationality dominates ... 'backstage', power and rationalization dominate ... actors' unwillingness to reveal rationalizations may be dangerous ... power often finds ignorance, deception, self-deception, rationalizations, and lies more useful for its purposes than truth and rationality ... (*ibid.*)

Flyvbjerg is saying that the power of rationality is weak, whereas the power that dominates can (more or less) get away with anything it wants and will even lie to achieve its ends. Notwithstanding, the two generally find a workable accommodation in stable relationships because, by and large, we prefer stable relationships to confrontation. But stable relationships can go wrong. Things that can make them go wrong include ignorance, deception and dishonesty on the part of the power that steadily dominates. And the reason we know that this power will deploy ignorance, deception and lies, among other tactics, is that reason and rationality, both weak and both fundamentally focused upon the reality of the lived experience, are on the receiving end. And it's the receiving end that we hear from as dissenters fight their hopeless corner. Why would they fight their hopeless corner if they were not trying to defend reality, if they were not fundamentally asserting the truth of what had happened? *Their* truth, *experienced* truth, not the rationality provided by power.

Once again, specific reference to the experience of the environmentalist, Rachel Carson, through the eyes of biographer and environmental historian, Linda Lear, is apposite:

> The hostile reaction of the establishment to Carson and her book was evidence that many ... officials realized that [she] had not only challenged the conclusions of scientists regarding the benefits of new pesticides, but that she had undermined their moral integrity and leadership.
> (Carson, 2000: 259)

Undeservedly but predictably, Carson was subjected to a torrent of untruths and abuse from all quarters which, reportedly, made her calmer and more determined still. And that is worth more than a moment's reflection if the solitary dissenter remains within your organisation as an apparent obstacle to its 'normal' functioning. Paradoxically, you marginalise and deride such people at your peril.

That same weakness of reason is what Case Study 1 found when the subject exposed the charade, delusion and deception of the official press releases issued in the days immediately after the flooding of King's Island. It is also what Flannery observed in the predicament of his Redemptorist superiors but rose above in his own resolve not to be brow-beaten. And, similarly, it is "the quiet decency and pragmatism of British conservatism" that Oborne sought to defend as his cherished *Daily Telegraph* was steadily torn apart by the profit motive. For Silone, the weakness must have lain rotting among the corruption of diverted post-earthquake relief aid – something validly *cafone*, a despicable lie to be trampled underfoot and kicked to one side out of the way.

But Flyvbjerg also warned that if we do not fashion ways of protecting the weaker opinion and the voice of reason, then things like ignorance, deception and lies can cause sudden confrontation. Once again, that is what Case Study 1 found when the subject called for decontamination and public health expertise on King's Island but the system ignored the plight of "fifty people in each of the two streets named" who were then in dire circumstances. Instead, the subject was told: "Close down your blog! *Get out!*" That is what drove Flannery and his friends when they founded the Association of Catholic Priests. And that is what Oborne so objected to when he discovered that his newspaper had buried the news that the Chinese government had gone so far as to refuse a delegation of British parliamentarians access to Hong Kong. But Silone *was* able to devise a protective measure. This would have emerged from the possibilities for dissent provided by civil disobedience – that is, dissent within the law. And his prescription did much, we understand, to rehabilitate him.

So, Flyvbjerg's exposure of 'democracy' in practice has cast very useful, supporting light upon the situation facing the lone, imminent dissenter and its implications for those involved in developments. A final observation on Foucault, who has done most of the work in Case Studies 2 and 3, may also provide a helpful round-up for the corporate reader, as well as a platform for comparison with Giddens for the more academic investigator.

The link between the two began with the origin of dissent. This was identified with ontological insecurity, which was defined as both a crisis of self-identity and a failure in the constancy of the individual's social and material environment for action (Giddens, 1990: 92). Ontological insecurity was triggered when external power cut across some "ultimate value or life meaning" (Löwith, 1993: 66) still preserved within the 'iron cage' of existence (Weber, 1930: 181). It is to that deeply felt intrusion that we return our attention now because the point of declaring dissent suggests that the burden of the 'cage' (with all its efficiencies, rational calculations and controls or, as we might put it today, with its digital technology, credit cards and ephemeral market fashions) has suddenly been completely eclipsed by an unbearable assault upon something else, an assault upon that elusive "ultimate value or life meaning". It is that ultimate value or life meaning that we need to pin down.

Foucault's excavation method has taken our investigation deeper than we managed to dig by ourselves: he has changed our understanding of what we thought had driven the expression of solitary dissent and exposed, in each of those case studies, a highly personal and not immediately apparent motivation. These motivations arose from 'a brutalising' of the *episteme* that Foucault referred to in that impossible sentence quoted in the Introduction – a no longer tolerable rupture of the conditions and boundaries for what can be imagined in a particular setting.

By *episteme*, Foucault was referring to "the orderly, 'unconscious' structures underlying the production of scientific knowledge in a particular time and place ... the 'epistemological' field which forms the conditions of possibility for knowledge in a given time or place" (*www.michelfoucault.com/concepts*). It is easy to 'think big' about *episteme*. Foucault himself envisages "a volume of space open in three dimensions" (2002: 378). In one dimension are the mathematical and physical sciences, in the second the empirical sciences, and in the third philosophical reflection. But he also explains that, in their various intersections, can be found "the various philosophies of life, of alienated man, of [concepts and problems]; ... those regional ontologies which attempt to define what life, labour, and language are in their own being; ... and lastly the formalisation of thought". It follows that it is also possible to 'think small' about *episteme* – to think more deeply about "the primary, irrefutable, and enigmatic existence of man" (as Foucault put it when considering the limits of the Classical *episteme* – *ibid.*: 338).

Note also, from that same difficult quote in the Introduction, how Foucault rejected where the modern *episteme* was heading ("its growing perfection") in favour of where it started ("its conditions of possibility"). 'Conditions of possibility' is a technical term meaning: the pre-condition for the knowledge under discussion; the structure which makes it possible to ground a discourse and glimpse 'domain' stripped of all its distorting, discursive practices; the fundamental assumptions ingrained within the consciousness found there.

That is what Foucault has helped us expose – and we can see how close this is to that "ultimate value or life meaning" at the core of ontological security that has suddenly been jolted. But Foucault, I believe, is 'genetically'[53] incapable of taking us deeper within the consciousness of individual as we have uncovered it at those points in Case Studies 2 and 3. By which I mean that Foucault's mind does not work in that way. He is more interested in 'the enterprise' than the fine detail: "[It, the enterprise,] is not so much a history, in the traditional meaning of the word, *but an 'archaeology'*" (*ibid.*: xxiv, italics added to reflect his inevitable sense of triumph). And the archaeology of knowledge was what inspired him, not the passions or prejudices or values or inhibitions of some individual. He loved uncovering things but, with that round of genuine applause, did not need to go any further.

---

[53] As indicated earlier in the book, I am using the expression in a convenient, non-specific, slangy sort of way.

Giddens, in contrast, did. And look at the difference.

In the example of Case Study 1, the subject followed the method drawn down from structuration theory, returning to the point of origin he still relished but had lost. He reconstitutes the rules and resources that shaped his upbringing and development and is able to describe a pattern of coherent, if rather untypical, professional and social experience until the duality of his existence suddenly broke down. But it is an intensely personal history of the duality of structure and agency that is being recounted, not abstracted conditions of possibility or a domain stripped bare of discursive practices. It's raw and real. We get under the skin of the subject. We even learn what his family called the 'loo'. And that is the way Giddens wants it: a pattern of recursively implicated social practice until suddenly the duality breaks down, the personal gyroscope begins to topple and the subject can no longer continue.

In the example of Case Study 4, the same thing happens. Giddens's method takes us on into Pescina itself, whereas Foucault left us having simply identified 'Abruzzo'. Once inside, we learn of the Christmas rituals and farmyard work, the types of food, the types of work and the realities of such education as was available:

> ... it was not a very stimulating life ... the most interesting things I learned on the street going back and forth to school. Even later, I must confess, what I learned, I learned from the street.
> (Pugliesi, 2013: 34)

We are told of the daily procession down through the town of goats, sheep, donkeys, mules cows, wagons of every description and peasants making their way down for the day's work. And then the weary trudge back each evening, exhausted. We even glimpse "the poor Christ, the suffering Christ, the peasant Christ who figures in the mythology of the rural poor" (*ibid.*: 3). We sit on the benches of the hometown of Pescina and think about the Church as distinct from Christ. We are reminded of the tragedy inherent in the town's human condition. We sense the sadness and hopelessness for ourselves. We remember the rigged trials and the unjustifiable sentences on those who stepped out of line with graft and organised crime. We are shown the significance of bread, wine, wolves, donkeys and water. And then, we count the seconds, thirty of them, when more than half the population was killed by the earthquake. And we dig mothers out of the ruins, including our own. Then we search for days for the other one who, miraculously, is still alive (although we have to clear the dirt from his mouth and nose ourselves). Yet life goes on as we shelter the herds and hear the wolves and smell their hunger and light the fires – and then eventually lose our brother, whom we could save from the mud but not from the men, and finally face the devastation of the exile where, broken and ill, we sink to the ground in dismay and desolation before the graft and corruption of those with power overall. The world of the Italian peasant was disappearing but not fast enough to leave Silone or the harsh rules and few resources of the Abruzzo unscathed.

And yet the young Secondino Tranquilli did, with the help of the mystic figure of Don Orione, manage to carve out sufficient space within that structure for an agency that would take him into betrayals, intrigues and prisons before he at last found his voice. And that voice spoke only truth, justice and compassion for the poor – not more of the same.

> Through their "intimate contact with animals and nature, through their direct experience of life's great events such as birth, love and death, many peasants acquire an immense wisdom."
> (*ibid.*: 36)

To those of us with imaginations but who have never faced such experiences, the patterns of recursive implication in Pescina leading to such 'immense wisdom' are profoundly disturbing. And Case Study 4 has shown us that you don't have to be a professor of sociology with a huge international reputation to devise a way of exploring them. Instead, your patient, lucid and accessible theorising gives shape, form, legitimacy and, crucially, the quality of being reproducible, to the equally patient but practically acquired, searching and sifting of others. And then, once again, it all breaks down and the subject has to declare his dissent.

There is only one more comparison to be made and it lies in the next Chapter – with Jean-Paul Sartre.

Chapter 9

Thoughts for the future

We have already seen that to declare dissent is transformational. The moral impact upon the dissenter is beneficial, although the practical consequence of saying "No!" may be rather different. Much would depend upon the degree of commitment he or she brings to the moment. Sartre urged maximum commitment – but he would, wouldn't he, because of the "conversional" quality (Mairet, 2007:19) of his intentionality or sense of Other. By which I mean, in Mairet's words, that Sartre is an 'evangelist', a 'proselytiser', a 'protagonist': by virtue of his consciousness, he must take responsibility. Foucault and Giddens, by comparison, are operating in quite a different context: one digs holes and struts the landscape he has just destroyed, while the other knits and crochets by the hearth of human existence working out exactly what happened. They both achieve freedom of a sort but there is no responsibility for humanity in their task. They are not existentialists. They are not like Sartre.

The dissenter who makes their point before quietly leaving may appear, in today's eyes, to have achieved more than them. But this is because today we expect conformity with the prevailing practices, not the unpredictability and risk of damage to established interests that a solitary campaigner might wreak. We can tolerate, even welcome, a mild hiccup of discontinuity if done with grace and style. It follows that the solitary dissenter who quietly leaves is like the person who talks of 'knowledge' in the singular: they are acquiescing in the prevailing discourse, not confronting its unwritten rules and assumptions and certainly not reaching for existential freedom. They may briefly have entertained and diverted but they have actually accomplished nothing and, existentially, let themselves down.

For solitary dissent to mean something, we are stuck with an outburst, with all its awkwardness, difficulties, frustration and anger, and we ourselves are committed to change and to accommodate it unless the interruption can be safely put down and hidden out of sight. Needless to say, the author of this book does not want discontinuity buried. Whether to do so is a judgement, therefore, with all its attendant risks, that those with power will have to face and take responsibility for. In this book, we can only begin to speculate at the shock-waves that will emanate outwards from someone suddenly standing up, saying "No!" and meaning it.

The first impact would appear to be upon civil society. We saw in Chapter 2 that, on approaching the moment of dissent, we found ourselves at a fork in the road but with the option, still, to turn back: behind us lay acquiescence and submission; to the front and on one hand, there was the 'in-betweenness' of a vibrant civil society and, on the other, the anguish of the solitary individual. If we take that latter path, there could be a consequence for civil society that has not yet been mentioned. The possible consequence can be highlighted by setting the solitary dissenter against civil society. Suppose that the individual has declared a convincing case of dissent while local civil society, presumably seised (or potentially seised) of similar issues, has not. If the solitary dissent has been effectively declared, then immediate doubts will be raised at the value of local civil society. Why have *they* not said anything? Is theirs an authentic civil society? What is wrong with its leaders? To what extent are they actually being controlled (see, for example, Keane, 1988: 6, and Cohen and Arato, 1992: 480) away from dissent and towards participation? To be sure, later questions about the solitary dissenter may be raised but they will be part of the risk-assessment process, not an exact reverse of the doubts streaming at civil society.

Arguably, therefore, a procedure could be set up to side-step the not uncomplicated and actually controversial mechanism of local people supposedly acting in free concert. But, equally, it is possible also to imagine a situation where solitary dissent could even be manipulated against other local interests. Perhaps the individual's delivery at the moment of dissent would give things away? Was it measured and rehearsed? Was this a real, spontaneous outburst of disbelief and rejection or something more considered? And if the latter, what has the dissenter actually considered, and with whom?

Evidently solitary dissent can be a dangerous area. A better response, therefore, might be to populate our governance, civil and corporate procedures with dissent-receptive, rather than dissent-resistant, mechanisms. That was the point raised in Chapter 2, drawn from Marcuse's pedagogic and Walzer's procedural dissent. There could be scope today, half a century later, for something altogether more sensitive and 'third way'.

'Third way' thinking was developed by Giddens (1988), consistently with a theory of generative politics, in response to excessively corporatist governance of society (see, for example, footnote 14 above). Giddens's purpose was to express pragmatically the ideological justification for dissent without the turmoil of rebellion – dissent that emanates within the public spaces that are created and occupied by citizens acting in concert[54] (Schechter, 2000: 96). Central to 'third way' politics is seeing the State as the enabler of new solutions – maintaining order through creating conditions which assure legitimacy for the radical measures necessary to modernise, overhaul and protect the national interest in a rapidly changing world. Necessarily, enabling new solutions for the State also entails enabling new relationships for its citizens. Power which accomplishes new relationships may be termed 'progressive' (Giddens, 2003) but Giddens's prescriptions were limited to "a strong public sphere, coupled to a thriving market economy; a pluralistic, but inclusive society; and a cosmopolitan wider world, founded upon principles of international law" (2003: 6) – not to accommodating solitary voices which jarred with the way the wind was blowing.

Alternatively, third level education (that is, college level) might incorporate the experience of dissent within its various social and political modules. The need might even be driven by the further effects of wholeheartedly deploying new teaching methods at first and second levels – for example, the experience being steadily introduced of students seeking information for themselves, sharing it and problem-solving it under the guidance of an experienced teacher[55]. Or perhaps, in a moment of enlightenment, third level education might direct its students at problem areas to make what they can of them – not to make what the colleges want them to make of them. The subject in Case Study 1 noted wryly that, despite the local University having an established research team at the site of the great Limerick Flood of 2014, none of its members was seen to turn up anywhere near the mud and distress of those affected. One stream of relevant activity, as a consequence, went completely unrecorded and unresearched (Kay, 2014: 32, 35) – and the flooded residents, in that particular respect, were completely unassisted.

---

[54] *Power to,* as opposed to *power over,* is another frequently encountered way of describing this sense of potential.

[55] An interesting example was quoted in *The Irish Times* of 12 January 2016, p.13, under the title *A teaching revolution that 'makes the classes come alive'.* The model came from Canada.

Or perhaps the solution lies at parliamentary level? The current Irish Dáil (parliamentary first chamber) has become synonymous with tight political party control and a refusal to give adequate accounts to questions raised. The popular belief is that the habit is growing. In an apparently Damascene, eleventh hour conversion in early January 2016, however, An Taoiseach agreed that henceforth the Speaker could be elected by secret ballot, which would serve to release power from the Government to the Oireachtas. Of course there are critics, not least the retired Oireachtas Clerk who suggests that this could be accomplished at the stroke of a pen rather than in the laborious, long-fingering, referendum-based way the Government is proposing. In other words, the conversion is all about all electioneering, not immediate action. Nevertheless, any step to strengthen the accountability of collectively representative fora must also be a sound step in the direction of protecting the solitary voice which says "No!"

Without measures such as these, however, it could transpire that the day of the dissenter is passing, because the nature of citizenship itself is changing.

Within a neoliberal and market-oriented 'competition State', citizenship can approach a condition of passive consumerism (Powell and Geoghegan, 2004: 27, citing Hertz; Cousins, 1996). There is a sense of obligation accompanying passive consumerism. It is to be a dutiful recipient of social benefits, to be a reliable source of tax receipts, and to exercise choice in accordance with the rules of the market (Marquand, 1997: 63). But this is clearly a denial of the starting point from which citizenship is traditionally measured – equality, freedom and potential – as well as a rejection of political, social and civil rights. It follows that the domination of the 'competition State' is wholly inconsistent with the potential of citizens no longer to consent.

The challenge for citizen interests seeking to uphold their freedoms and to fulfil their potential to stop consenting is more than just the decision whether to reject the 'competition State' or to engage with it. It is equally more than a question of trusting enough in the institutions already present to accept that new rules and forms of governance will somehow accommodate citizen unease. The challenge is that trying to defend citizen interests – for example, by objecting to the actions of dominant projects – can carry heavy costs while offering no obvious course of action either.

On the one hand, immersion in activities recommended or approved by the State is, by the act of consent, in the nature of denial of *political* citizenship (Powell and Geoghegan, 2004: 16): it lends legitimacy to the projects of the State (Meade and O'Donovan, 2002: 4): and will tend to diminish the authenticity of whatever condition civic culture happens to find itself in. On the other, rejection of such activities necessarily entails adopting a radical political alternative, which may come at a heavy price (Powell and Guerin, 1997: 144, citing the example of reduced availability of funds for local development initiatives). The central difficulty remains, however, that habitually not engaging with the State – in other words legit-imising its excesses by default – is to degrade the means of successfully rejecting them. This is a circular dilemma of a different order to the ten-sions normally associated with civic culture which is what habitual en-gagement understands. *Political* citizenship, which is intrinsic to citizen-ship status, cannot function without a pre-existing civic culture. At the same time, the institutions of *social* citizenship, which are the means of resisting passive consumerism, become rigid and possibly overbearing in the absence of active or *civic* participation (Marquand, 1997: 152). In ef-fect, the degraded institutions of social citizenship work against the po-tential of political citizenship in the absence of a civic culture. Through conformity, moreover – for example in fashions, life-styles and employ-ment practices (see, for example, Brown, 2004: 383) – citizens are increas-ingly demonstrating that being *socially* true to themselves has less influ-ence over their ability to act than do the economic expectations of the State and the trends of the market. In further effect, it becomes increas-ingly and quickeningly less challenging to acquiesce in the State and the market than to object to the actions of dominant interests. A degraded form of *social* citizenship then becomes a means by which dominating projects can continue to dominate and shape the public imagination.

Without a healthy civic culture and the citizen habit of regular partici-pation (in order to contest as opposed to acquiescing), without protection, without intervention, how is the voice of dissent going to be heard tomor-row?

There is a glimmer of hope. It originates in a characteristically existen-tialist way and has a humanist luminosity about it. The fact remains that people will still declare their dissent when something repellent affronts them, regardless of the exigencies of social and political citizenship. The city of Cologne in Germany showed us as much in the early hours of New Year's Day, 2016, when it was reported that gangs of male asylum-seekers had molested, in an organised way, hundreds of women celebrating the New Year in the city centre. The extraordinary consequence of that un-pleasant development was, within just a week or two, that a Police Chief had resigned, that a national policy of taking refugees wholesale had been cast off the rails, and that German right-wing gangs were hunting out refugees and taking their revenge. Dangerous stuff indeed. But, unusually, Cologne was also a case of *collectively* declaring around 500 *solitary* voices of dissent. So, perhaps civil society can help the solitary dissenter if mechanisms of solidarity and communication can be overhauled, reimagined and widely embraced.

Then think also of Paris again, that city that has pulsed steadily in the background of this exploration of standing up and being different. The year 2015 took us from the 'Charlie Hebdo' experience in January, through to the attacks on St Denis and the Bataclan Theatre, and the empty pairs of shoes in La Place de la République in November. It is not rogue jihadists the Parisians were dissenting from but what they had done to Parisian friends and neighbours who could no longer express the word "No!" themselves.

If we are to survive and, struggling, reach for freedom in this world – a world which is under threat from climate change as much as from extremists and unrestrained capitalism – we need as a society to be able confidently to justify our *collective preparedness to be outraged for others*. We need to be ready to share mutual anguish, to take responsibility for it and to show others that we are doing so. We need to underwrite it, as participants wholly opposed to all forms of malpractice, corruption and violence, to replicate it in our social interaction, and to demand that everyone listens when the lone voice speaks out. We need recursively to implicate it in the societies we hope to build tomorrow and, genealogically, to dig it out again and again whenever someone else's oppressive reconstitution of the facts attempts to bury it or otherwise efface it from humanity. We need to wear that badge of intentionality on our coat lapels and in our hatbands – places where we can never forget them, like yellow stars stitched on to the rags that yesterday's totalitarianism left for those who were considered sub-human[56]. And we need to begin to articulate the one absolute truth underpinning it all, that our individual sense of self and

---

[56] There is the true story that the King of Denmark, who used to ride out early in Copenhagen's parks in the 1930s and 40s, also wore a star on his coat on the same morning that all Jews in Denmark were ordered by the Nazis to show stars on their coats – another memorable act of dissent.

humanity will be honoured and defended in every gathering of free citizens.

This is perhaps where philosophies of conscience, like existentialism, which seemed consigned to yesterday, can re-forge that link between people in concert and people alone. May we all pray for the solitary voice of dissent – and for our ability to continue hearing it.

"Not in our name! Not in mine! *No!*"

Bibliography

Adshead, M., 2006. "New Modes of Governance and the Irish Case: Finding Evidence for Explanations of Social Partnership", *The Economic and Social Review*, 37(3), 319-342.

Arendt, H., 1973a. *Crises of the Republic*. Harmondsworth: Pelican.

Arendt, H., 1973b. *Men of Dark Times*. Harmondsworth: Pelican.

Arondson, R., 2013. Introduction, in *We only have this life to live: the Selected Essays of Jean-Paul Sartre 1939-1975*, R. Arondson and A. Van Den Hoven (eds.), New York Review Books.

Bennet, A., and Royle, N., 1999. *An Introduction to Literature, Criticism and Theory*, 2nd Edition. Hemel Hempstead: Prentice Hall Europe.

Brown, T., 2004. *Ireland: A Social and Cultural History, 1922-2002*, London: Harper Perennial.

Caldwell, R., 20067. Agency and Change: Reevaluating Foucault's Legacy', in *Organization*, Vol. 14(6), London: Sage.

Carson, R., 2000. *Silent Spring*. London: Penguin Classics.

Clegg, S., 1997. 'How to become an Internationally Famous British Social Theorist', in *Anthony Giddens: Critical Assessments*, C.G.A. Bryant and D. Jary (eds.), pp139-158, Routledge: London and New York.

Clegg, S., 2000. Power and Authority, Resistance and Legitimacy, in *Power in Contemporary Politics: Theories, Practices, Globalizations*, H. Goverde, P. Cerny, M. Haugaard and H. Lentner (eds.), 77-92, London: Sage.

Cohen, D., 2005. "How I nearly became a terrorist", *Dissent*, Spring 2005.

Cohen, M., 2002. "An Empire of Cant", *Dissent*, Summer 2002.

Cohen, M., 2014. "The Values of Dissent", *Dissent*, Winter 2014.

Cohen, J., and A. Arato, 1992. *Civil Society and Political Theory*, Cambridge Mass.: MIT Press.

Corra, M., and D. Willer, 2002. "The Gatekeeper." *Sociological_Theory*, 20(2), 180-20

Cousins, M. 1996. "The Quality of Public Services: Clarifying Conceptual Issues", *Administration*, 44(4), 83-92.

Cushman, T., 2004. 'Anti-Totalitarianism as a Vocation', *Dissent*, Spring 2004.

Daly, S., 2007. "Mapping civil society in the Republic of Ireland", *Community Development Journal*, Advance Access published online 31 January 2007, doi;10.1093/cdj/bs1051.

Dostoevsky, F., 1849. Letter, cited on http://www.fyodordostoevsky.com/biography.php

Drake, R., 2009. *Ignazio Silone: The Assault on a Cultural Icon*, on the Humanities and Social Sciences on-line Net, https://www.h-net.org/reviews/showrev.php?id=25624.

Fairclough, N., 1995. *Critical Discourse Analysis: The Critical Study of Language*. London: Longman.

Faux, J., 1977. "In an African Prison: A Memoir", *Dissent*, Fall 1977.

Flannery, T. (Anthony), 2013. *A Question of Conscience*. Dublin: Londubh Books.

Flynn, T., 2006. *Existentialism: A Very Short Introduction*, Oxford: Oxford University Press,

Flyvbjerg, B., 1998. *Rationality and Power: Democracy in Practice*. Chicago: University of Chicago Press.

Foot, J., 2000. *The Secret Life of Ignazio Silone*, New Left Review, May-June, 2000.

Foucault, M., 1972. *The Archaeology of Knowledge*. London: Tavistock Publications.

Foucault, M., 1998. *Aesthetics, Method, and Epistemology*, Vol. 2, J. Faubon (ed.), London: Allen Lane, Penguin Press.

Foucault, M., 2002. *The Order of Things*, Oxford: Routledge.

Fox, N., 1998. "Foucault, Foucauldians and Sociology." *British Journal of Sociology* 49(3), 415-433.

Giddens, A., 1984. *The Constitution of Society*, Cambridge: Polity Press.

Giddens, A., 1987. *Social Theory and Modern Sociology*, Cambridge: Polity Press.

Giddens, A., and Pierson, C., 1998. *Conversations with Anthony Giddens: Making Sense of Modernity.* Cambridge: Polity Press.

Giddens, A., 1990. *The Consequences of Modernity*, Stanford, Ca.: Stanford University Press.

Giddens, A., 2003. Introduction. Neoprogressivism: A New Agenda for Social democracy, in *The Progressive Manifesto: New Ideas for the Centre-Left*, A. Giddens (ed), 1-34, Cambridge: Polity.

Gitlin, T. "The Culture of Celebrity", *Dissent*, Summer 1998.

Gordon, C., 1980. *Power/Knowledge: Selected Interviews and Other Writings, Michel Foucault.* New York: Pantheon.

Goverde, H., Cerny, P., Haugaard, M., and Lentner, H., 2000. General introduction, in *Power in Contemporary Politics: Theories, Practices, Globalizations*, H. Goverde, P. Cerny, M. Haugaard and H. Lentner, (eds), 1-34, London: Sage.

Gray, A., 1998. Management, Accountability and Public Sector Reform, in R. Boyle and T. McNamara. (eds), *Governance and Accountability: Power and Responsibility in the Public Service*, Dublin: Institute of Public Administration.

Gutting, G., 2001. *French Philosophy in the 20th Century*, Cambridge: Cambridge University Press.

Haskell, G.K.,1982. "Roger Baldwin, 1884-1981", *Dissent*, Winter 1982.

Haugaard, M., 2000. Power, Ideology and Legitimacy, in *Power in Contemporary Politics: Theories, Practices, Globalizations*, H. Goverde, P. Cerny, M. Haugaard and H. Lentner, Eds, 59-76, London: Sage.

Haugaard, M., 2016. 'The Constitution of Power', in *The Journal of Socio-Economics* 27.6., Academic OneFile.

Judd, H., 1975. 'A Spontaneous Upsurge of Dissent in India', *Dissent*, Summer 1975.

Kay, M., 2009. *Public Private Partnerships: The Challenge of Accountability, Stewardship and Legitimacy.* Unpublished Doctoral Thesis, University of Limerick.

Kay, M., 2014. *The Limerick Flood of 2014: Climate Change and a Case of Unpreparedness*. Dublin: OriginalWriting.

Keane, J., 1988. *Civil Society and the State*. London: Verso.

Levi, J., 1975. "Political Prisoner in Cuba", *Dissent*, Summer 1978.

Lourie, R., 1972. "When to Leave the Country", *Dissent*, Summer 1972.

Lourie, R., 1974. "Soviet Dissidents & the Balance of Power", *Dissent*, Winter 1974.

Löwith, K., 1993. *Max Weber and Karl Marx*, T. Bottomore and W. Outhwaite (eds). London: Routledge.

Lukes, S., 2005. *Power: A Radical View*, 2nd edition, Basingstoke: Palgrave Macmillan.

Luxemburg, R., 1940. *The Russian Revolution*, Chapter 6 "The problem of dictatorship", New York: Workers Age Publishers, www.marxists.org/archive/luxemburg/1918/russian-revolution/ch06.htm

Mairet, P., 2007. "Introduction", in *Jean-Paul Sartre: Existentialism and Humanism*, Jean-Paul Sartre, trans. P. Mairet, York: Methuen.

Marcus, D., 2015. "Into the Cave: Sheldon Wolin's Search for Democracy", *Dissent*, Fall 2015.

Marquand, D., 1997. *The New Reckoning: Capitalism, States and Citizens*, Cambridge: Polity Press.

McNay, L., 1994. *Foucault: A Critical Introduction*. Cambridge: Polity Press.

Meade, R., and O. O'Donovan, 2002. "Editorial Introduction: Corporatism and the ongoing debate about the relationship between the state and community development." *Community Development Journal*, 37(1), 1-9.

Medina, P, 2015. "The Courage of the Poet", *Dissent*, Fall 2015.

Mills, N., 1983. "Power Chic as Style and Politics", *Dissent*, Fall 1983.

O'Broin, D., and Kirby, P., 2009. *Power, Dissent and Democracy: Civil Society and the State in Ireland*, (eds.), Dublin: Farmar.

O'Farrell, C., 2005. *Michel Foucault*, London: Sage.

Palmer, I.S., 2001. "Florence Nightingale: Reformer, Reactionary, Researcher" in *Nursing Issues in the 21st Century: Perspectives in the Literature*, E.C.Herd (Ed), pp. 26-38, Philadelphia: Lippincott Williams & Wilkins.

Penttinen, E., 2000. "Capitalism as a System of Global Power", in *Power in Contemporary Politics: Theories, Practices, Globalizations*, H. Goverde, P. Cerny, M. Haugaard and H. Lentner, Eds, 205-220. London: Sage.

Powell, F., and Geoghegan, M., 2004. *The Politics of Community Development*, Dublin: Farmar.

Powell, F., and D. Guerin, 1997. *Civil Society and Active Citizenship: the role of the voluntary sector*, University of Ulster (Coleraine): Association for Voluntary Action Research in Ireland.

Pugliesi, S., 2009. *Bitter Spring*, New York: Farrar, Straus and Giroux.

Sartre, J-P., 2007. *Existentialism is a Humanism*, Yale: Yale University.

Sartre, J-P., 2013a. "A Fundamental Idea of Husserl's Phenomenology: Intentionality", in *We only have this life to live: The Selected Essays of Jean-Paul Sartre 1939-1975*, R. Arondson and A. Van Den Hoven (eds.), pp.3-6, New York Review Books.

Sartre, J-P., 2013b. "Introducing *Les Temps Modernes*", in *We only have this life to live: the Selected Essays of Jean-Paul Sartre 1939-1975*, R. Arondson and A. Van Den Hoven (eds.), pp.129-145, New York Review Books.

Sartre, J-P., 2013c. "Existentialism: A Clarification", in *We only have this life to live: the Selected Essays of Jean-Paul Sartre 1939-1975*, R. Arondson and A. Van Den Hoven (eds.), 86-91, New York Review Books.

Sartre, J-P., 2013d. "The Liberation of Paris: An Apocalyptic Week", in *We only have this life to live: the Selected Essays of Jean-Paul Sartre 1939-1975*, R. Arondson and A. Van Den Hoven (eds.), 115-118, New York Review Books.

Sartre, J-P., 2013e. "Merleau-Ponty", in *We only have this life to live: the Selected Essays of Jean-Paul Sartre 1939-1975*, R. Arondson and A. Van Den Hoven (eds.), 310-383, New York Review Books.

Schechter, D., 2000. *Sovereign States or Political Communities? Civil society and contemporary politics.* Manchester: Manchester University press.

Sheridan, A., 1980. *Michel Foucault: The Will to Truth.* London: Tavistock Publications.

Siedelman, R., 1989. "The Short Sweet Song of Chinese democracy". *Dissent*, Fall 1989.

Silone, I., 2006. "Notes from a Swiss Prison", *Dissent*, Summer 2006.

Sinavsky, A., 1984. "Dissent as a Personal Experience", *Dissent*, Spring 1984.

Sleeper, J., 1983. "Black Politics in Brooklyn", *Dissent*, Spring 1983.

Walzer, M., 2013. "Feminism and Me", *Dissent*, Winter 2013.

Weber, M., 1930. *The Protestant Ethic and the Spirit of Capitalism*, London: Unwin.

Zweig, S., 1964. *The World of Yesterday*, University of Nebraska Press.

Index

www.ingramcontent.com/pod-product-compliance
Lightning Source LLC
Chambersburg PA
CBHW070925270326
41927CB00011B/2729